MY LOVE

PETER CHUNG
ILLUSTRATIONS BY: WINDEL EBORLAS

Order this book online at www.trafford.com
or email orders@trafford.com

Most Trafford titles are also available at major online book retailers.

© Copyright 2018 Peter Chung.
Author of the Selected Poems of Korean Minstrel Kim Sat Gat

Print information available on the last page.

ISBN: 978-1-4907-9188-3 (e)
ISBN: 978-1-4907-9189-0 (sc)

Library of Congress Control Number: 2018913089

Our mission is to efficiently provide the world's finest, most comprehensive book publishing service, enabling every author to experience success. To find out how to publish your book, your way, and have it available worldwide, visit us online at www.trafford.com

Any people depicted in stock imagery provided by Getty Images are models, and such images are being used for illustrative purposes only.
Certain stock imagery © Getty Images.

Trafford rev. 11/05/2018

www.trafford.com
North America & international
toll-free: 1 888 232 4444 (USA & Canada)
fax: 812 355 4082

My Love

Peter Chung

To my eternal sage and wife, Amie

Preface

My Love contains 128 poems for my wife, Amie, who departed this life fifteen years ago. I have been in forty-six countries, and photos of the various places were taken to sketch their ambiences. Some of them are included in this book to help readers respond to the poems. *My Love* has a special drawing on the last page Amie made reminiscing about our fifth wedding anniversary in 1981. I hope *My Love* would help people transform their enmity into goodwill.

2018

Acknowledgments

The poems I have written are for Amie, my wife, who is the universe to me. My deepest appreciation must go to Amie, who drenches me in her celestial and never-ceasing love and tenderness. The drawings in this book are Amie's. Without her love and drawings, it would never have been possible for me to complete *My Love*.

CONTENTS

I. HOME

RAIN AND CHERRY BLOSSOM[1]

Thou art my certain lifesaver,
Renewing my desolate heart.
Thou art my passionate lover,
Caressing my face without art.

Thou art my subtle musician,
Burnishing me on the petal.
Thou art my dancing magician,
Making my falling twirl vital.

Thou art my perspective painter,
Dropping my petals to dress earth.
Thou art my lifetime messenger,
Foretelling my beaming rebirth.

Thou art my eternal soul mate,
Being merged in earth at our date.

비와 벗꽃

그대 나의 확실한 구조자,
나의 황폐한 마음 새롭게 하는
그대 나의 열렬한 연인,
나의 얼굴 꾸밈없이 어루만져 주는

그대 나의 미묘한 음악가,
나의 꽃잎 빛나게 하는
그대 나의 춤추는 마술사,
나의 낙하 공중제비 생기 불어넣는

그대 나의 풍경 화가,
나의 꽃잎 떨구어 대지 수놓는
그대 나의 생애 전령,
나의 기쁨 넘친 부활 예시하는

그대 나의 영원한 영혼의 반려자,
우리의 만남에 대지 스며드는

THY EYES[2]

Thy eyes are starlit,
Hiding Vega's brilliance,
Twinkling at the zenith of heaven,
Reviving my tattered soul, quickened
With sapient winks lighting my path.

Thy eyes are starlit,
Holding Buddha's benevolence,
Transforming into morn dews at dawn,
Rescuing my fettered soul, enlivened
With genial gazes guiding my path.

---

[2] Composed on August 26, 2015.

그대 눈망울

그대 눈망울 별빛,
직녀성 눈부심 감추고
하늘 천정에서 반짝이며
내 헤진 영혼 소생시켜 살게 하고
슬기로운 눈짓으로 나의 길 밝혀 주는

그대 눈망울 별빛,
부처 자비심 담고
새벽 아침 이슬로 나타나
내 갇힌 영혼 구제하여 생기 주고
따스한 눈길로 나의 길 보여주는

YEARNING[3]

A gentle breeze, thou saith.
Azure, thy quilt unfolded.
Aroma from sweetbriers, thy breath.
Azalea petals, thy lips parted.

Peach blossoms in springtide, thy demureness.
Lightening in sultry summer, thy celerity.
Scarlet leaves in autumn, thy devotedness.
White snow in yuletide, thy chastity.

Purling of a rivulet, thy voice.
Violets in leas, thy color.
Frothy splashes of waves, thy resilience.
Morning glory, thy valor.

A resplendent dew in the morn is thy beginning
And flaming heavens in gloaming, thy ending.

---

[3] Composed on October 10, 2015.

그리움

온화한 산들바람 님 말함
쪽빛 하늘 님 펼쳐 논 이불
해당화 향기 님 숨결
진달래 꽃잎 님 내민 입술

봄날 복숭아꽃 님 정숙함
찌는 여름 번개 님 기민함
가을 새빨간 잎 님 열정
크리스마스 흰 눈 님 순결

시냇물 소리 님 목소리
들판 세비꽃 님 색깔
거품 파도 철썩 님 여일함
나팔꽃 님 꿋꿋함

눈부신 아침 이슬 님의 시작
황혼의 불타는 하늘 님의 마침

IRIDESCENT LOVE[4]

At the first sight, a fiery storm
Nearly engulfed the fledging love.
Narrowly escaping Hades,
In a loving hut, we played house.
Near the railroad harbored younglings.

At a hilltop nestled lovers,
At Koeun nest as newlyweds,
At Lafayette as explorers,
In Long Island as seafarers,
In Chuncheon as a unity.

In Oakland, half left for Lethe.
The partner in pitch-dark despair,
Mourning for one hundred eight days,
Had a sweet dream at Cressington
Right on the one hundred twelfth day,
Half resurrected to hug me,
No longer in grief but bliss.

---

[4] Composed on September 28, 2015.

무지개 빛 사랑

첫눈에 격렬한 폭풍
갓 피어난 사랑 거의 삼켜 버렸지
염라대왕 만남 가까스로 벗어나
사랑의 오두막에서 우린 소꿉놀이 하다
기차길 옆 젊은이로 살았지

언덕배기 연인으로 자리잡았지
고은 보금자리 신혼으로
라피엣 탐구자로
롱 아일랜드 뱃길 여행자로
춘천 한 몸으로

오클랜드에서 반쪽 레테로 떠났지.
배우자 칠흑 같은 절망 속에
108일 동안 슬퍼하다
바로 112일째
크레싱톤에서 달콤한 꿈 꾸었지.
그 반쪽 부활하여 나를 껴안아
더는 슬픔 없이 환희에 차 있네

COSMOS[5]

Elongated frail necks
In autumn sky, craned
In an unruffled breeze,
Are all ready to gleam.

Eight aesthetic faces
In pink, red, white, imbued
Even in a faint sunshine,
Are delighted to beam.

---

[5] Composed on October 17, 2015.

코스모스

기다란 가녀린 목
가을 하늘로 빼어
잠잠한 미풍에도
기꺼이 빛나는

여덟 꽃잎 얼굴
빨강, 분홍, 하양으로 물들어
희미한 햇살에도
반가이 미소 짓는

CHRISTMAS TREE[6]

With Amie's ethereal art,
Christmas tree's embellished yearly,
With Santa Claus making a dart
Or climbing, angels with holly
Or playing as Muse, carts finished,
Glass candles, and bulbs in red, blue,
Silver, green, and gold, replenished
With delight of our wedding hue.

In my lighthearted hastiness,
Christmas tree is timely settled
With golden bells in vividness
And Santa on dolphin straddled.

Jovial carols are jingling
And cheerful lightbulbs gamboling.

---

[6] Composed on December 13, 2015.

크리스마스트리

아미의 천상의 솜씨로
매년 장식되는 크리스마스트리
돌진하거나 기어오르는 산타,
호랑가시나무 가지 들거나
뮤즈처럼 연주하는 천사,
세련된 마차, 유리 양초,
빨강, 황금빛, 은백색, 초록, 파랑 전구로
우리 결혼식 빛깔의 기쁨 채우면서

나의 명랑한 성급함으로
때맞춰 마련뵌 크리스마스트리
밝은 황금 종, 돌고래에 걸터앉은 산타로

캐럴 즐겁게 울려 퍼지고
전구들 유쾌히 뛰어 노네.

CIEL BLEU[7]

The heavens reveal their own way.
Crispy air wafts in knolls and vales
And brooms shadowy dust away;
Young branches long for spring in vales.

Amie's sixtieth birthday draws
Near, January 26,
Forty-one years after the day
Of our holy matrimony,

Hundred forty-seven months fleeting
In her cozy omnipresence,
Bliss of Amie's birth exuding
And exposing her quintessence.

Sing a love descant to Amie
To extol her true love to me.

---

[7] Composed on January 4, 2016.

파란 하늘

하늘은 속내 드러낸다.
서늘한 기운
언덕과 골짜기에 스며
탁한 먼지 쓸어 내니
골짜기 어린 가지 봄 기다리네

아미 60세 생신
1월26일로 다가와
우리 신성한 결혼식날 이후
41년

아미 아늑한 편재 속에
147개월 지나가지만
아미 탄생의 환희 물씬 풍기며
그녀 진수 드러내네

아미에게 사랑의 한 곡조 노래하리
나에 대한 그녀 참사랑 찬미하려

WINTER NIGHT[8]

Orion trumps the kindred feast;
Next to Polaris Cepheus,
King of Ethiopia comes
With his wife Cassiopeia
And his daughter Andromeda,
Fallen to Cetus's offering
By her mother's hubris only,
Evoking all young men's daring,
Rescued by Perseus timely.

Orion's charm and bravery
Won Artemis's affable heart,
But he's doomed by her archery,
Fooled by Apollo's crafty art,

With hounds completing for hunting
To prepare just for reveling.

---

[8] Composed on January 7, 2016.

겨울 밤

오리온
가족 향연 알리니
북극성 옆 케페우스 이디오피아 왕,
아내 카시오페아,
딸 안드로메다와 함께 나오네

어머니의 오만함 만으로
바다 괴물 시터스 제물 되었지만
뭍 젊은 남성들의 대담함 일으키며
때맞춰 페르세우스가
구출한 안드로메다

매력과 용맹으로
아르테미스의 우정 일었지만
아폴로의 간교에 속은
그녀의 궁술에 쓰러진
오리온

사냥개 함께 사냥하려 내달리며
단지 향연 준비하네

Constellations: Cepheus (top); Cassiopeia (middle); Andromeda (bottom). Photo was taken on January 19, 2016, at Hwacheon Chou Kyong Chol Astronomical Observatory. The brightest star on the top left is Polaris.

SONG FOR SILVER GRASS[9]

In the fall breeze of refreshment,
Supplely dancing silver grass,
Frozen and with snow daubed,
Longing for new heydays.

In the winter adornment,
Stilling silver grass,
In memories deep engrossed,
Pining for glittering days.

---

[9] Composed on January 23, 2016.

억새

상쾌한 가을 바람에
유연하게 춤추던 억새
얼어 눈 덮여서도
새로운 한 때 기다리며

겨울 장식 속에
멈추어 있는 억새
추억 속 깊이 빠져
눈부신 날 갈망하며

DOUBLE RAINBOW[10]

Brief rainfall, dousing
Scorching, sultry air,
Squeezing sweat off pores
And slackening arms,
Releases tension
Even in August's ire.
Two rainbows brushing
The azure's stair
And a fleece of clouds
With the beaming charms
Prelude Ascension,
Drawing closer here.

[10] Composed on September 5, 2016.

쌍무지개

순식간 비
구멍마다 땀 방울 쥐어 짜고
팔 무력케 하는
태우는 듯한 찌는 대기 식히고
8월 분노에서도
긴장 덜어주네

쌍무지개
하늘 계단, 양털 구름
눈부신 매력으로 붓질하며
승천의 날 여기
더 가까이 다가온다고
미리 알리네

MISSIVE[11]

From thy wildflower, Amie,
In love—forever
To my ○○○○ Longed in Universe, Thine,
Surpassing things of this world,
Longed, morn star in my heart!
I love you! Forever!
Matter is but bits of paper.
Just with thy cherished love,
This universe will be
Ever filled, all with bright stars.
For thy aspiration,
Ready, go!

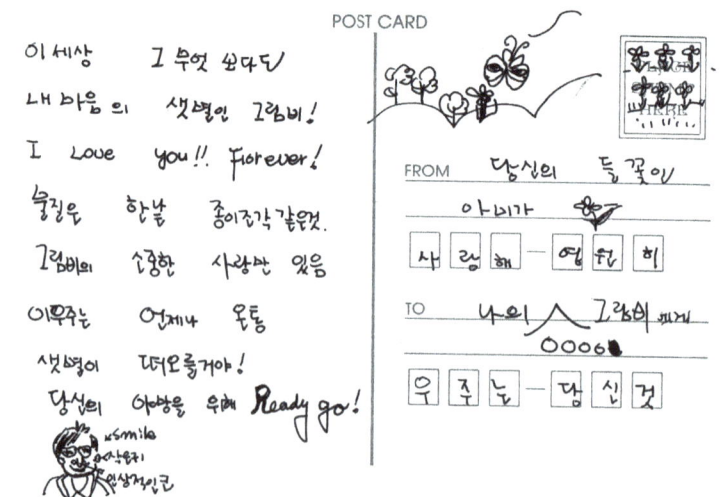

---

[11] Postcard written by Amie in 1986.

서신

당신의 들꽃인 아미가
사랑해-영원히 나라에서
우주는 당신 것인
나의 ○○○○ 그림비에게
이 세상에 그 무엇보다도
내 마음의 샛별인 그림비!
물질은 한낱 종이조각 같은 것.
그림비의 소중한 사랑만 있음
이 우주는 언제나 온통
샛별이 떠오를 거야!
당신의 야망을 위해 Ready go!

SERYANG-JE[12]

I'm going to Lake Seryang-Je
To meet a hidden world, glimpsing.

Mist arising early morning
And spreading into the water
Shows the world endlessly changing.
Never the same in Seryang-Je!

I'm going to Lake Seryang-Je.

[12] Photo taken on April 29, 2017, at Seryang-Je in Hwasun, Jeollanam-do, Korea.

세량제

나 가네 세량제
얼핏 보이는 숨은 세상 만나려

이른 아침 일어나는 안개
물 속으로 퍼져 나가면
세상 쉼없이 변하는 것 보여주지
세량제 똑 같지 않아, 언제나!

나 가네 세량제

RECUMBENT BUDDHA'S DREAM[13]

Thousands of Buddhas and thousands
Of towers stood at Unjusa.

Hundreds of Buddhas and towers,
And temples greet visitors now.

At the sunset mound lies Buddha,
Dreaming to rise in a new world
And enlighten people to reach
Neither ills nor pain nor aging.

---

[13] Photo taken on April 28, 2017, at Unjusa Temple in Hwasun, Jeollanam-do, Korea.

와불의 꿈

천불천탑 서 있던 운주사

이젠 수백의 불상과 탑, 그리고 절
오는 사람 반기네

석양 언덕에 누워있는 부처
새로운 세상에서 일어나
사람에게 깨달음 주어
병들지 않고
고통받지 않고
늙지 않길
꿈꾸고 있네

ODONGDO CAMELLIA[14]

Our call without camellia bloom,
Quickening the beats to rapture,
The lone call in bloom without thee,
On the ground arranging A-M-I-E,
One by one with fallen flowers,
Sensing thee palpable to loom.

[14] Photo taken on April 8, 2017, at Odongdo Island, Yeosu, Jeollanam-do, Korea.

오동도 동백

동백꽃 없을 때 우리 방문
고동 빨라지며 환희에 젖었고,
꽃 필 때 님 없는 외로운 들름
떨어진 꽃 하나하나 가지런히
땅 위에 아미 적으니
아렴히 떠오르는 님 느끼네

II. AFRICA

A LITTLE WONDER[15]

Mind-boggling scenes unfold in Chobe.

Elephants crossing the river,
Tranced by sweet grass in the islands,
Slowly walk into the water;
In the deep float the whole bodies,
With the trunks stretched forward and tails
Up straight out of water, and swim,
Blowing water out of the trunks.

What a marvel such giants float;
What a guide savory fare is!

---

[15] Photo taken on August 6, 2014, at Chobe National Park in Botswana.

작은 놀라움

놀라운 광경 초베에 벌어지네

강 건너는 코끼리
섬의 달콤한 초원에 취하여
천천히 물속으로 들어가다
깊은 곳에 온 몸 띄우네
코 앞으로 내 뻗고
꼬리 물 밖으로 꼿꼿이 세워
코로 물 내뿜으며 헤엄치네

저 거대한 몸집 뜨는 것 신기하고
맛있는 음식 대단한 길잡이여!

SONG OF REED[16]

Mokoro glides on waterways
With rustling reeds and lilies
Over Okavango Delta.
At the stern stands a boatman with
A long pole, steering to reeds,
Pauses at a scene amid sky,
Water and song of reeds, led
To oneness with Okavango.

[16] Photo taken on August 8, 2014, at Okavango Delta in Botswana.

갈대의 노래

모코로 미끄러지듯
바스락 거리는 갈대,
수련으로 덮인
오카방고 델타 물길 나아가네

선미에 선 뱃사공
긴 장대로 갈대 속으로 나아가다
한 폭 그림에 멈추면
하늘, 물 그리고 갈대의 노래
오카방고와 하나되네

FATED MIGRATION[17]

Countless herds of wildebeest end
Last feast and start the migration
For a feast on the savanna
Anew, ready after rainfall,
Across the dark Mara River,
Waiting for the hapless, dire doom,
Joined by drowning or crocodiles;
On the carcasses roost vultures
And marabous having a feast.

[17] Photos on page 40 taken on August 8, 2014, at the Maasai Mara National Reserve in Kenya.

숙명적인 이동

수 많은 누 무리
마지막 향연 끝내고
이동을 시작하지
사바나에 비 온 뒤
새로 마련된 향연 찾아

불운한 누에겐
익사나 악어로 이어지는
참혹한 운명 숨어있는
어두운 마라 강 건너

사체엔
독수리, 대머리 황새 자리잡고
향연 만끽하지

Maasai Mara National Reserve in Kenya

Mara River

MAURITIUS[18]

The blue and the blue on the edge
Tête-à-tête tell a tale of old;
The dodo, flightless and rampant,
Walked on the island but long gone,
Leaving bones, stories, and riddles.
The dodo breathes alive in farce,
Mauritius polymer notes, coins,
And Alice in the wonderland.

---

[18] Photo taken on August 9, 2008, in Mauritius.

모리셔스

푸른 하늘 파란 바다
저 끝 머리 마주 앉아
옛날 이야기하네
날지 못하지만 흔하던 도도
섬 돌아다녔지만
오래전 사라졌다고
뼈, 이야기, 수수께끼 남긴 채
도도 살아 숨쉬고 있지
익살, 모리셔스 지폐와 동전,
이상한 나라의 알리스에서

SOCIAL BIRDS[19]

Arid climate and scarce water,
Never cease their lively babbling
At the large communal dwelling,
Together weaved with twigs and thatch.

The bustling commune delivers
How well the social devoir works
To uplift our sociableness.

---

[19] Photo taken on August 10, 2014, in the Kalahari in Namibia.

44

사회적인 새

메마른 풍토와 물 부족도
결코 멈추지 못하지
잔가지와 풀로 함께 엮은
그 커다란 공동 주택에서 벌어지는
그들의 활기찬 수다를

번성하는 공동체
자신들의 사회적 의무
얼마나 잘 이행되는지 보여주며
고양시키지
우리들 사교성을

RED DUNE[20]

Dune 45 lies with the head
To the right and the lissome spine,
Enduring wind brooms, and garners
Five-million-year-old sand powdered;
Sunrise on the back transforms dunes
With sharp blades, dissecting scarlets
And shadows to the surreal;
That lasts only for a moment.

---

[20] Photos on page 48 taken on August 11, 2014, in the Namib Desert in Namibia.

붉은 사구

사구 45
오른 쪽으로 머리 두고
날렵한 등줄기 보이며
지속되는 바람이 쓸어 모은
빻아진 오백만 년 모래

그 등에서 일출
예리한 날 세운 사구
선홍색과 음영으로 나누며
초현실 세상으로 바꾸네
단지 한 순간동안 남아 있는

Dune 45 in the Namib Desert

Scene at the sunrise on Dune 45

DEADVLEI[21]

No droplet escapes the dead marsh,
Encircled by reddish sand dunes;
Camel thorns stand scorched as phantoms.
At the foot of a dune is life,
Green camel thorns thriving with clumps;
The burning thirst, soothed with morn mist,
Revives the phantoms to beauty.

[21] Photo taken on August 11, 2014, in the Namib Desert in Namibia.

데드블레이

물방울도 벗어나지 못하는
그 죽은 습지사구
불그스레한 모래 사구에 둘러 쌓여
아카시아 햇볕에 그을린 채
환영으로 서 있네

한 사구 기슭에 삶
덤불과 함께 살아 있는 푸른 아카시아
그 불타는 갈증
아침 안개로 달래고
그 환영
아름다움으로 소생시키네

CAPE OF GOOD HOPE[22]

Emerald sea lullabies sand
Veiled in white on the Dias beach;
The white lighthouse on craggy rocks
Overlooking the blue foaming
Complements the Cape of Good Hope.
How many seafarers found hope
Instead of storms wrecking clippers?
All's mesmerized, its ageless hope.

[22] Photo taken on August 15, 2014, at the Cape of Good Hope in South Africa.

희망봉

에메랄드 바다,
디아스 해변
흰 베일 두른 모래에
자장가 들려주고
험한 바위 위 흰 등대
포말이는 바다 내려다보며
희망봉 만드네

얼마나 많은 뱃사람
빠른 범선 난파시킨 폭풍
대신 희망 찾았나?
모두 매료되는 것,
영원한 희망이야

TABLE MOUNTAIN[23]

Devil's Peak turns against Table
And blurts, "No mount without its peak!"
Mountain smiles peace with evenness
Where fade apartheid and hatred;
Overlooking on the table,
Vista molded for long eras
And stretched far to the Atlantic
Stirs calmness to delight renewed.

[23] Photo taken on August 16, 2014, in Cape Town, South Africa.

테이블 마운틴

데블스 피크
테이블에 등 돌리며 내뱉는다
"봉우리 없는 산 없지!"
마운틴 한결같은 평온 미소 짓네
그 한결같음에
차별이나 미움 빛 바래지

오랜 세월동안 빚어 낸
멀리 대서양까지 펼쳐진 풍광
테이블에서 바라보면
평온함 움직이며
새로운 즐거움 주지

KILIMANJARO[24]

Kibo away from Mawenzi,
Over the cloud, draws the gaze glued
On its snow, recalling Harry,
A writer with desire barren,
And the frozen leopard corpse in
The Snows of Kilimanjaro.
Never in vain waste the longing.

---

[24] Photo taken on July 29, 2014, in Moshi, Tanzania.

킬리만자로

키보
구름 위
마웬지와 떨어져서
시선을 끌어
자신의 눈에
달라붙게 하며,
킬리만자로의 눈 속
보람없이 욕망만 가진
작가 해리
그리고 그 곳
죽어 얼어붙은 표범
되살아나게 하네.
열망 꼭 헛되지 않게 하소서

STONE TOWN[25]

The Old Fort, walled with gray corals,
Greets outlanders warmly as friends.
Close by stands the House of Wonders,
White as coral and three storied,
Asking a riddle on wonders.
They're electricity and lift.
Tinge, interwoven with colors,
Arabic, Portuguese, English,
Cloaks Stone Town without much ado.

[25] Photo taken on July 25, 2014, in Stone Town in Zanzibar.

스톤 타운

올드 포트
잿빛 산호로 둘러 쌓여
이방인 따뜻이 친구처럼 맞이하네

산호처럼 희고 삼층으로 된
하우스 오브 원더스
놀라움에 대한 수수께끼 내며
가까이 서 있네

그건 전기와 승강기

아랍, 포르투갈, 영국
색깔들 엷게 섞이며
큰 소동없이 스톤 타운 덮네

WHIPPING POST[26]

Men, women, and children were brought
To the slave market. Men tied to
The post were priced by harsh whipping:
Sooner, moaning lowered the price.
Livingston's appeal to free slaves
Turned the market to the Christ Church,
And altar displaced Whipping Post;
His heart was buried nigh the tree,
A crucifix hung on the wall.

---

[26] Photo taken on July 25, 2014, in Stone Town in Zanzibar.

채찍질 기둥

남자, 여자, 아이들
노예시장에 끌려 나와
남자 기둥에 묶어
가혹한 채찍질로
몸 값 정했지
신음 빠르면
값 떨어진다는

리빙스턴
간절한 노예 해방 바람
그 시장
그리스도 교회로
채찍질 기둥
제단 되고
그 심장 묻어 던 곳 나무
십자가 되어 벽에 걸렸네

NUNGWI BEACH[27]

Fishers fixing nets for morn catch
Merge into emerald and white;
Clouds shroud above the coral reefs.

Craggy cliffs jut out over white,
Dazing my eyes under noon rays
To the azure over the jades.

Dhows glide on ripples tinted with
Red rays and somber jades at dusk.
Peerless delight and sensation!

---

[27] Photo taken on July 27, 2014, on a dhow in Zanzibar.

능귀 해변

아침 고기잡이 위해
어망 손질하는 어부들
에메랄드, 하양 어우러지네
산호초 위 구름 덮여 있는데

울퉁불퉁한 절벽
튀어 나와 하양 위
한낮 햇살에 눈부셔
비취 위 창공으로 눈 돌리네

다우 미끄러져 가네
황혼 붉은 빛과 어두운 비취로
물들인 물결 위를,
기쁨과 감흥 견줄 바 없네!

VICTORIA FALLS[28]

O behold Mosi-oa-Tunya!

Zambezi flows into a chasm;
Her muteness thunders to the smoke,
Engrossing the soul and body;
Rainbows arise from the ravine,
Filling the world with hope and love.

---

[28] Photos on page 66 taken on August 5, 2014, in Zambia and Zimbabwe.

빅토리아 폭포

오, 보라 모시 와 투냐!

잠베지 계곡으로 흘러 들며
그녀의 말없음
천둥소리 내며 연기로 변하네
영혼과 육체 빼앗으며
무지개 골짜기에 피어나
희망과 사랑으로 세상 가득 채우네

Victoria Falls viewed in Zambia

Victoria Falls viewed in Zimbabwe

BAOBAB[29]

A giant takes a child in me
To the home of the little prince,
Removing baobab timely
And the secret of the tamed fox:
The essential is visible
Just with the heart, not to the eye.
The giant unharmed draws water
From the deep to nourish neighbors.

---

[29] Photo taken on August 5, 2014, in Zimbabwe.

바오밥

거인 내 안의 아이 데려간다
때 맞춰 바오밥 뽑아 내는
어린 왕자의 고향
그리고 길들여진 여우의 비밀로,
가장 중요한 것은
가슴으로만 볼 수 있지
눈에 보이지 않는다는,
상처받지 않았던 거인
깊은 곳에서 물 길러
이웃 살지게 하네

III. AMERICAS

PIER 39[30]

Amie used to spend hours and tell
The scattering site for her ash
Half the way between Alcatraz
And Pier 39, scattering
Handfuls of her ash to touch on
The textured surface to gold dust,
Dancing down with the rays, dazzling
My eyes to eternal bliss and
Whispering, "I'm ever with you."

30 Photo taken on October 3, 2017, at Pier 39 in San Francisco, United States.

72

피어 39

아미가 시간을 보내면서 곧잘 말하던
그녀 재 뿌려 달라던 곳
앨카트래즈와 피어 39 중간
그녀 재 한줌씩 뿌리면
그물 펼쳐진 수면 만나
황금 티끌로 변해
빛과 춤추며 내려가며
내 눈 눈부시게 하여
영원한 천국의 기쁨으로
속삭이네
"난 늘 당신과 함께 있어"

KILAUEA[31]

Burning desire to see the blue,
Opening the old scars again,
Crossing roads and rushing to her,
The desire scorching the ocean
To steam and clouds and cooling off,
Never ending till none is left.

---

[31] Photo taken on December 19, 2005, in Hawaii, United States.

킬라우에아

푸르름 보고픈 불타는 욕망
옛 상처 다시 벌려
길을 건너 그녀에게 달려가네

그 욕망 바다 태워
수증기, 구름 만들고 진정되네
끝없이 그 욕망 다할 때까지

MAKAPUU BEACH[32]

Manana Isle, cute as a calf,
Searching for Mom in the ocean,
Barrels breaking on sandy beach,
A lighthouse on the precipice,
Beaconing the reefs off the bay,
A day on the beach fleeting by.

---

[32] Photo taken on December 21, 2005, at Makapuu Beach in Oahu, Hawaii.

마카푸우 해변

바다로 엄마 찾는
고래새끼처럼 귀여운 마나나 섬

모래해변에 부서지는
밀려드는 파도

만에 흩어져 있는 산호 알려주는
절벽 위 등대

해변에서 하루 순식간 지나가네

NIAGARA FALLS[33]

The Horseshoe, American, and
Bridal Veil make Niagara
Majestic, graceful, and virgin,
Sonorous and harmonious;
Pleasure and pragmatism couple
In the Falls done for charm and force.

[33] Photo taken on October 2, 2017, at the Skylon Tower in Niagara Falls, Ontario, Canada.

78

나이아가라 폭포

호스슈
아메리칸
신부의 베일
나이아가라
장엄하고
단아하고
순결하게 만들어
격조 높게 조화롭네

매력과 위력 위해
다룬 폭포
오락과 실용 하나되네

GRAND CANYON[34]

Aeonic epic, unfolding
On the stage of the Grand Canyon,
Lightens the visual cortex
To impart timeless scenes to me;
Vishnu rocks to Kaibab limestone,
Unraveling two billion years.

그랜드 캐니언

그랜드 캐니언 무대 위 펼쳐진
영겁의 서사시
시각 피질을 밝혀
영겁의 장면 내게 전하네,
비쉬누 암석 카이밥 석회암에게
20억년 이야기 들려주는

LADY AURORA[35]

How many days passed to see Aurora!
Freed from the official choirs of two years,
With sleepless nights to wish one fair weather,
Thinking the places to meet the Lady,
To Fairbanks, I went in February.

With a camera bought for Aurora,
Late arrival wiped out one of six nights;
The second night, with the thick clouds disturbed,
My patience dried up till two in the morn,
Then showing a faint glimpse of the Lady.

The third night revealed dainty Aurora
With deep emerald and pale reddish hues;
The fifth night with the majestic Lady,
Dancing and mesmerizing all the night,
Lightened all the heavens till early dawn.

---

[35] Composed on February 22, 2017. Photos on page 84 taken on February 16, 2017, at Cleary Summit in Fairbanks, Alaska, United States.

레이디 오로라

얼마나 많은 날 보냈었나,
오로라 보기위해!
두 해 동안 붙매였던 일 벗어나
단 하루 좋은 날씨 바라며
잠 못 이룬 밤들
레이디 오로라 만날 곳
깊이 생각하며
나는 이월 페어뱅크스로 갔네

오로라 위해 카메라 사 들고
늦은 밤 도착으로
여섯 밤 중 첫 밤을 잃고
둘째 밤 두껍게 뒤덮인 구름
나의 인내 어지럽혀
새벽 두 시까지 메마르다
레이디 언뜻 보여주었네

셋째 밤 맵시 있게 드러낸 오로라
짙은 에메랄드, 옅은 빨강 색조로
다섯째 밤 레이디 장엄하게
춤추며 눈부시게 온 밤 매혹시키며
온통 하늘 이른 새벽까지 밝혔네

Photo taken at Cleary Summit in Fairbanks

Photo taken at Cleary Summit in Fairbanks

BIRCH HILL[36]

Willowy birches lined on snow,
Opening a scene of Cezanne's
With a trail for Nordic skiing,
Evergreen spruces befriended
And revealed become a backdrop.

Who else would be right in the scene?
A soul with the aesthetic sense
And love embellishing the world;
Birches awning over the snow
Tinge the universe all in white.

[36] Composed on February 26, 2017. Photo taken on February 17, 2017, at Birch Hill in Fairbanks.

버치 힐

날씬한 자작나무
눈 위에 모여 열린 세잔 화폭
노르딕 스키 오솔길
늘 푸른 가문비 친구 삼아
배경 드러내네

그 장면에 걸 맞을 다른 누구 있을까?
그 심미안과 사랑으로
세상 장식할 영혼
눈에 드리운 사작나무 차양
온 우주 하얗게 물들이네

BARILOCHE[37]

A man mounting a horse stands on
The graffitied ROCA platform,
Boldly at the Civic Center,
Facing the Nahuel Huapi
In teal blue, posing a riddle.
From his Conquest of the Desert,
Was the death of the Indians!

[37] Photo taken on March 3, 2014, at the Civic Center in Bariloche, Argentina.

바릴로체

말 탄 남자
짙은 청록의 나우엘 우와피
마주하는 도시 센터에
낙서가 된 ROCA주춧대 위
당당하게 서있다
수수께끼 자아내며

그의 사막정복으로
인디인들의 죽음이 있었기에!

PERITO MORENO GLACIER[38]

Perito Moreno Glacier,
Wide enough to cover three miles
And long to extend nineteen miles,
Expands in Argentino Lake,
Orchestrating a cycle of
Dam, ice bridge, and rupture in turn
To overwhelm viewers with awe
In climate change–shrinking glaciers.

---
[38] Photo taken on March 5, 2014, in the Los Glaciares National Park in Argentina.

페리토 모레노 빙하

페리토 모레노 빙하
넓어서 3마일 덮고
길어서 19마일 펼쳐져
아르헨티노 호수에 퍼지네

댐, 얼음 다리 그리고 붕괴
차례로 연출하며
보는 사람 경탄으로 압도하네
빙하 줄어드는 기후변화 속에서도

USHUAIA[39]

The Land of Fire owns Ushuaia,
Bulwarked by the snow-clad mountains
Facing south the Beagle Channel;
On the way to the Atlantic,
Les Eclaireurs greets the feathered,
Keeping all sails out of harm's way.

---

[39] Photo taken on March 9, 2014, in Ushuaia, Argentina.

우수아이아

불의 땅의 우수아이아
눈 덮인 산으로 보호 받으며
남쪽으로 비글채널 마주하고 있네

대서양 가는 길
레제클레러르 새들 반기며
모든 항해 안정하게 지켜주네

WHAT PICASSO DIDN'T! [40]

A signboard of an atelier
Enigmatically saying,
"What Picasso didn't paint is here!"
Calls anyone to find the clue.

Under a blue awning outside,
Quaint drawings come effortlessly
From strokes of a man in the hat,
Guillermo Alio, well-known,
Right to tangos of La Boca;
He tangos with his partner on
Canvas painting by steps in tune
To marvel what Picasso didn't,

---

[40] Photo taken on March 11, 2014, at La Boca in Buenos Aires, Argentina.

피카소가 못한!

"피카소가 그리지 못한 것
여기 있다" 정체 모를
이야기하는 아트리에 간판
누구든지 불러 그 답 찾으라 하네

밖의 푸른 차양 아래
기묘한 그림들
모자 쓴 남자
널리 알려진 기에르모 알리오
그의 필치에서 손쉽게 나와
바로 라 보카 탱고 되네

그와 파트너, 캔버스 위에서
탱고 추며 장단 맞춰
발자국으로 그려 낸 놀라움
피카소도 못한

EVITA[41]

La Recoleta is adorned
With tales, tragic or inspiring,
"FAMILIA DUARTE" decked
With twelve plaques just for Evita
And bouquets and flowers showing
Argentine deep veneration
Of Evita, very alive
In the hearts of the Argentine.

[41] Photo taken on March 11, 2014, at La Recoleta in Buenos Aires.

에비타

라레꼴레타
슬프거나 고무적인
이야기로 꾸며졌지
"파밀리아 두아르테"
바로 에비타 위한 열두 개 명판과
꽃다발, 꽃들로 장식되어
아르헨티나인들의 마음 속에
분명 살아있는 에비타에
깊은 존경 보여주네

IGUAZU FALLS[42]

Quaffing half the Iguazu,
The Devil's Throat thunders to mist,
Turning to clouds in the azure;
The other half unfolds curtains,
Inviting boats to its courtyard,
Soaking all with awe and rapture.

---

[42] Photos on page 100 taken on March 13, 2014, at Iguazu Falls in Argentina.

이과수 폭포

단숨에 이과수 절반을 삼키며
악마의 목구멍
천둥 치며 나온 안개
창공 구름 되네

다른 절반 장막을 펼치고
안뜰로 유람선 초대하여
경외와 환희로 모두 적시네

Devil's Throat of the Iguazu Falls in Argentina

Iguazu Falls in Argentina

CHE GUEVARA[43]

Metal scrap recycled becomes
Che Guevara in El Alto,
Near La Paz of Bolivia,
Where captured and executed,
Standing on an eagle, charging
As a revolutionary
Wayfarer to utopia.

[43] Photo taken on February 21, 2014, near La Paz in Bolivia.

체 게바라

재활용된 고철
잡혀서 처형되었던 볼리비아의
라파스 근처 엘 알토
체 게바라 되어
독수리 밟고 서서 돌진하네
이상적 세상 찾아가는 혁명의 여행자처럼

SALAR DE UYUNI[44]

Isle covered with giant cacti
Floating on the sea froth–ridden
Clouds only on the horizon,
Discerning the froth and white salt.

Mount Tunupa married Kusku,
Eloping with sly Kusina;
Tears and milk in feeding her child,
Being Salar de Uyuni.

44 Photo taken on February 23, 2014, at Salar de Uyuni in Bolivia.

104

살라르 데 우유니

커다란 선인장 덮인 섬
포말 가득한 바다에 떠있고
수평선 구름만은
포말과 흰 소금 분별하네

투누파 산 결혼한 쿠스쿠
은밀한 쿠시나와 눈 맞아 달아나
눈물과 아이 먹일 때 젖
살라르 네 우유니 되어라

ÁRBOL DE PIEDRA[45]

Time after time, wind blows with sand,
Carving rock for long to a tree
Christened Árbol de Piedra,
The left hand raised up to the sky
Allowing the palm visible,
Asking a question, "What is this?"
Better titled Left Hand of Zen
"Mano Izquierda de Zen."

---

[45] Photo taken on February 24, 2014, in the Eduardo Avaroa Andean Fauna National Reserve in Bolivia.

아르볼 데 피에드라

몇 번이고 모래 바람
오랫동안 바위 조각하여 나무 만들어
아르볼 데 피에드라라 부르네

하늘로 치켜든 왼손
그 손바닥 보인 채
질문하네
"이 뭣고?"
더 잘 지은 이름, 참선의 왼손—
마노 이스끼에르다 데 센

FLAMINGO[46]

Dropping their heads to Laguna,
The flamingos scoop red algae,
Knowing the secret of the lake
To brighten the plumage in pink;
Loving to be immersed in flocks,
The flamingos fly off to calm,
Sprinting a few steps to the air
To dazzle in their chic beauty.

---

[46] Photos on page 110 taken on February 24, 2014, at Lagunas Cañapa and Hedionda in Bolivia.

플라밍고

라구나에 머리 내려뜨리고
플라밍고 붉은 말 떠올리네
깃털 분홍으로 빛낼 수 있는
호수의 비밀 알고서

무리 지어 몰두하기 좋아하는
플라밍고 조용한 곳으로 날아가네
몇 걸음 질주하여 하늘로
우아한 아름나움 눈부시게

Flamingos at Laguna Cañapa in Bolivia

Flamingos at Laguna Hedionda in Bolivia

THE REDEEMER[47]

Opening two arms for world peace,
Standing on Mount Corcovado
And overlooking the Rio,
Christ the Redeemer embodies
The cross to redeem man from sin,
Cleansing the wrong to the righteous.

---

[47] Photo taken on March 15, 2014, in Rio de Janeiro, Brazil.

구세주

세계평화 위하여 두 팔 벌리고
코르코바도 산에 서서
리오를 바라다보고 있는
그리스도 구세주
인간을 죄에서 구제하는
십자가 구현하네
그릇된 자 바르게 정화시키는

IPANEMA[48]

Blue-green ocean, white sand and surf,
Added to Hill of Two Brothers,
Make Ipanema enthralling,
Bossa Nova to sing a girl,
Young, tan, and charming, to arouse
Exclamations and sighs in there.

[48] Photo taken on March 16, 2014, in Rio de Janeiro, Brazil.

이파네마

청록색 바다, 하얀 모래
그리고 밀려드는 파도
두 형제 봉우리와 만나
이파네마
보사 노바 매료시켜
그 곳에서 탄성과
한숨 나오게 하는
젊고 태양에 그을린 매력적인
여자아이 노래하네

SAN PEDRO DE ATACAMA[49]

The Valley of the Moon expands
Amphitheater, silky dunes,
Three Marias, labyrinths, and
More on Atacama Desert,
The sunset on Coyote Rock
Evoking the spirit of Mars.

[49] Photo taken on February 25, 2014, in San Pedro de Atacama, Chile.

116

산페드로 데 아타까마

달 계곡 펼쳐 놓네
원형극장, 비단 같은 사구,
세 마리아, 미로들, 더 많은 것
아타까마 사막에

코요테 바위에서 해넘이
화성의 혼 불러일으키네

VALPARAÍSO[50]

The amiable seaport known
As Little San Francisco and
A port of call for sailing to
The Atlantic from Pacific
Embraces La Sebastiana
On the hillside for Neruda,
Satiating eyes looking out.

[50] Photo taken on February 28, 2014, at La Sebastiana in Valparaíso, Chile.

발파라이소

작은 샌프란시스코와
태평양에서 대서양으로
향해위한 기항지로 알려진
온후한 항구
언덕배기에 네루다 위한
라 세바스티아나 껴안고 있네
내려다보는 눈
실컷 만족시키며

PETROHUÉ FALLS[51]

The white volcano Osorno
Sits between Todos Los Santos
and Llanquihue with Petrohué,
Mingling the white froth with blue green
And trolling all in unison!

---

[51] Photo taken on March 1, 2014, at Petrohué Waterfalls in Chile.

페트로우에 폭포

하얀 오소르노 화산
토도스로스산토스와
얀키우에 사이 앉아있네

그 흰 포말, 청록색에 섞으며
다 같이 돌림노래 부르는
페트로우에와 함께!

TORRES DEL PAINE[52]

Torres charm in shining armor
The daring like Agamemnon
For millions of years, cooling down
The fiery passion under earth
To arise in haughty calmness;
Emerald offers Lake Pehoé.

---

[52] Photo taken on March 7, 2014, at Torres del Paine National Park in Chile.

토레스 델 파이네

토레스 은빛 갑옷입고
아가멤논처럼
대담한 자 매료시키지
수백 만년동안
활활 타오르는 땅 밑 열정 식히고
도도한 냉정으로 솟아
에메랄드 페오에 호수에 바치네

PUNTA DELGADA[53]

The Strait of Magellan, parlous
To cross, heralds a sound between
The Delgada and Land of Fire,
Buses, cars, and trucks in long queues
Waiting long hours for its mercy.

---

[53] Photo taken on March 8, 2014, in Punta Delgada, Chile.

푼타 델가다

건너기 위태로운 마젤란 해협
델가다와 불의 땅 사이
최단거리 알려주고

버스, 자동차, 트럭 길게 늘어서
오랫동안 그의 자비 기다리네

LAGO GREY[54]

The glacier, freeing his pieces
Into Lago Grey to turquoise
Floes in turbidity and wind,
Measuring my absurdity
To dip my bare feet in the Grey
And chill a child smiling in me.

---

[54] Photo taken on March 7, 2014, at Grey Lake in Chile.

라고 그레이

빙하 자신 살점
그레이 호수로 떼어내
탁함과 바람 속 터키석 유빙으로

맨발 그레이에 담그고
내 안에 웃고 있는 아이 얼리는
나의 어리석음 재어 보네

MIRAFLORES[55]

El Beso, of two lovers hugged
In a fervid kiss at the park
Overlooking the sea below,
Moves on a raft at the sunset,
Telling that Dios es Amor.

---
[55] Photo taken on February 13, 2014, in Lima, Peru.

미라플로레스

두 연인 껴 앉고
뜨거운 키스 나누는
엘베소

바다 내려다보이는 공원에서
석양노을 뗏목 위로 움직이며
신은 사랑이라 하네

ICA[56]

Dune sandboarding, titillating;
Buggy ride, electrifying;
Huacachina, refreshing;
The fun time, unnoticed, passing.

---
[56] Photo taken on February 14, 2014, in Ica, Peru.

이까

사구 모래 타기 흥 돋고
버기카 타기 짜릿하며
우아카치나 상쾌하여
그 재미있는 시간 가는 줄도 모르네

BALLESTAS ISLANDS[57]

On the way to Ballestas Isles,
The Candelabra geoglyph,
Engraved on the slope by trenching
Sand as Viracocha's trident,
Emits an esoteric mood.
An isle sits like a centipede,
Some isle with caves or pebble beach,
Paradise for guanays and seals.

---

[57] Photos on page 134 taken on February 14, 2014, at Pisco Bay and the Ballestas Islands in Peru.

바예스타스 섬

바예스타스 섬 가는 길
경사면에 모래 파서
비라코차 삼지창처럼 그려 놓은
칸델라브라 상형그림
은밀한 분위기 내놓지

지네처럼 앉아있는 섬도 있고
어떤 섬 동굴이나 자갈 해변 있어
가마우지, 물개들 전국이지

Paracas Candelabra at Pico Bay in Peru

Ballestas Islands near Paracas in Peru

NAZCA LINES[58]

Man, hummingbird, monkey, spider . . .
Glyphs sprawl on the arid plateau,
Casting the never-ending whys,
Some answered in cosmology,
Some in religion or culture,
Or else the spaceman refuted.
More yet to come, asking more whys.

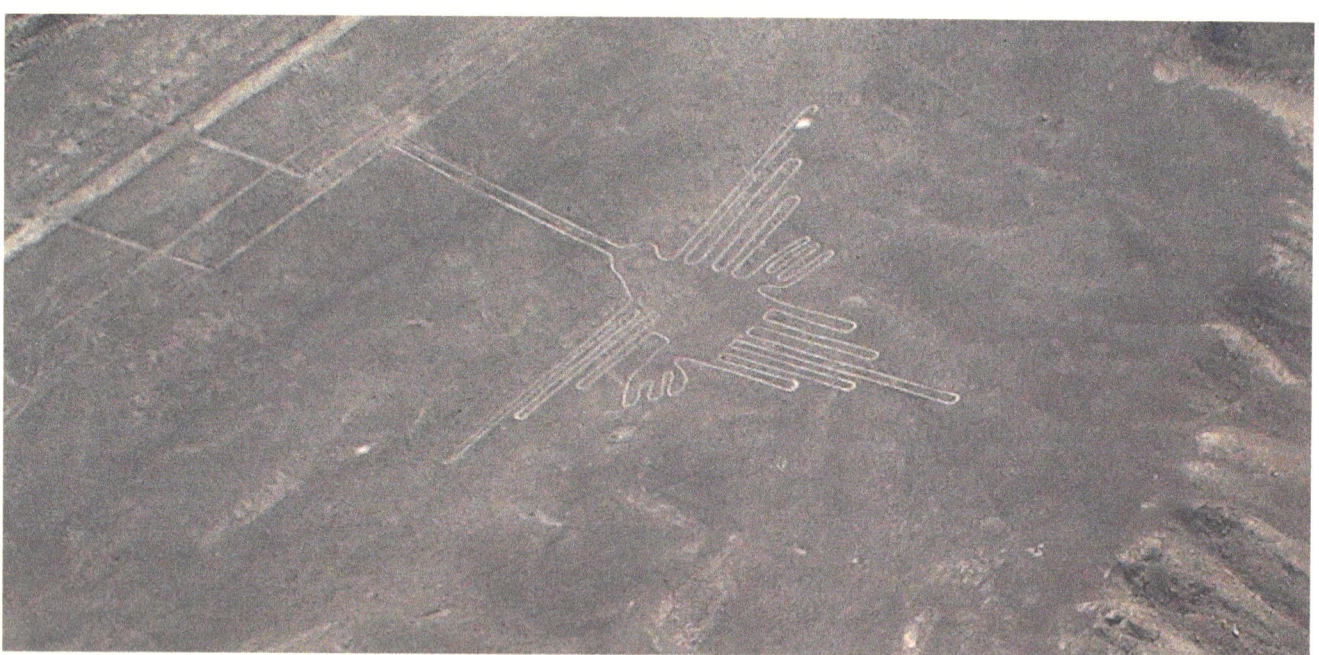

---

[58] Photo taken on February 15, 2014, over the Nazca Desert in Peru.

나스카 라인

사람, 벌새, 원숭이, 거미...
그림들 메마른 고원에 누워
끊임없는 의문을 던지지
어떤 이 천문으로 답하고
어떤 이는 종교나 문화로
아니면 우주인, 반박 받은
아직 더 나올 그림들
까닭 더 물으며

CHAUCHILLA TOMB[59]

Leaning on a wall of mud bricks,
A thousand-year-old femme, entombed,
Mummified with her hair intact,
Sits in red raiment and weaved quilt;
Earthen potteries with a gourd
Tell a piece of her daily life.

[59] Photo taken on February 15, 2014, at Chauchilla Cemetery in Peru.

차우치야 무덤

진흙 벽돌 벽에 기대
천년 동안 묻힌 여자
머리카락 그대로 미라 되어
붉은 옷 입고
실로 짠 이불 두르고 앉아있고
토기 그릇, 바가지
일상 한 단편 말해주네

OLLANTAYTAMBO[60]

Viracocha, next to storage
Looking down Ollantaytambo,
Saw twists and turns of the Inca
With Pumatallis terraces
And the Sun Temple unfinished,
Yielding her queen to Pizzaro.

---
[60] Photo taken on February 17, 2014, at Ollantaytambo in Peru.

오얀따이땀보

창고 옆 비라꼬차
오얀따이땀보 내려다보며
푸마딸리스 테라스와
짓다 만 태양신전 있는
잉카의 우여곡절 지켜보았네
자신들 여왕
피자로에게 넘겨 버린 걸

MORAY[61]

Moray displays Inca ruins
With circular terraced platforms,
Puzzling in the structure and shape,

With the temp gaps of terraces,
Crops of different seasons sowed,
Together at right terraces?

[61] Photo taken on February 19, 2014, at Moray in Peru.

모레이

모레이 잉카유적 보여주네
원형 테라스 층계로 되어 있는
당혹케 하는 그 구조와 모양

층계사이 온도차이로
계절 다른 작물 씨앗
그에 맞는 테라스에 함께 뿌렸나?

DODECAGONAL STONE[62]

The dodecagonal stone used
In walling an Inca palace,
Posing for the archbishop now,
Telling the wondrous masonry
Tightly fitted with no mortar
And greeting crowds in the alley.

[62] Photo taken on February 19, 2014, in Cusco, Peru.

12각형 돌

잉카 궁전 담에 쓰였던
12각형 돌
이제 대주교 위해 자리잡고
모르타르 없이도 단단히 맞추는
놀라운 석공술 이야기하며
그 골목의 인파 맞이하네

LAKE TITICACA[63]

Titicaca, vast enough to
Hold Peru and Bolivia,
High to straddle on the Andes,
Said to give birth to the Incas
And with scores of floating islands
Of totora mats Uros made.

---

[63] Photo taken on February 20, 2014, in Peru.

티티카카 호

티티카카
광대하여 페루와 볼리비아 차지하고
높이 안데스에 앉아
잉카 탄생시켰다며
우로스 만든 토토라 매트로
띄워 만든 섬 수십이네

IV. ASIA

A LITTLE KILEPEM[64]

To buy some bookmarks, she's cajoling me
With stardust wafting o'er her shiny eyes,
In two score of years warmly known to me
As profusely shed Amie's limpid eyes;
To get a few in treading Chime's stupa
Was released right away in my whisper.
There're local fiends under a stupa,
Subdued by Lama Kunley's phallus force;
In front of a large manicha turning,
Kilepem waited for my arrival.
Which two and why I should buy, I whispered.
Two were chosen with her swift approval,
Three balloons and a rose in two colors,
Mama, Papa, and her: Bhutan's colors.

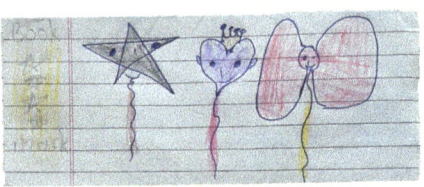

---

[64] Bookmarks Kilepem chose for me at Chime (Chimi) Lhakhang in Bhutan on August 20, 2017.

어린 킬레펨

책갈피 사달라며 날 졸라 대며
반짝이는 두 눈 매력 풍기네
사십 년간 따스이 내게 알려진
아미 해맑은 눈망울이
가득 내놓는 그 매력처럼

치미사원 탑 둘러본 후
몇 개 사주겠다고
곧바로 속삭였지
탑 아래
램 쿠엔리 성기의 힘으로
제압당한 지방 요괴들

돌고 있는 커다란 마니차 앞에
킬레펨 내가 오길 기다렸지
어느 것 두개, 왜 사야 하는지 속삭이자
순식간 두개 선택했지

세개의 풍선 그리고 두 색깔의 장미
풍선은 엄마, 아빠와 그녀
색깔은 부탄의 색이라고

KILLING FIELDS[65]

Mute screams reverberate in a stupa
From thousands of skulls, shattered or tortured;
Outside are sprawled pits altered to mass graves.
Haunting about a pit paled in bamboo
Are four hundred fifty victims perished
By hoe, hatchet, and other ruthless tools;
A Chankiri tree writhes in screeching ghosts
Of children smashed against its trunk and dumped
Into pits near corpses of their parents.
What an uncivilized insanity
Just from discord in ideas or stocks!

---
[65] Photo taken on November 24, 2017, at Choeung Ek in Cambodia.

킬링필드

맞아 부서지거나 고문 당한 수천 해골
그 소리 없는 절규
불탑내에서 울려 퍼지고
밖에 널려 있는 집단 무덤 된 구덩이들

대나무 울타리로 둘러 쌓인 구덩이
떠나지 못하는 사백 오십 영혼들
괭이, 손도끼, 다른 무자비한 연장에 스러진

몸부림 치고 있는 찬키리 나무 한 그루
자신의 몸통에서 부셔져
부모 시신 가까이 내버려진 아이들
그 유령들 비명속에서

얼마나 야만적 미친 짓인가,
단지 생각이나 민족성이 다르다고!

TA PROHM[66]

The solemn Ta Prohm, weighted by ages,
Wears cloak in greenish blue and pale yellow,
Fettered by flourishing Atlas's children,
Striving along to hold up the heavens.
Monks of old gathered to recite scripture;
Now people crowd only for view capture.
The monks' zeal is dimmed in visual joy.

---

[66] Photo taken on November 25, 2017, at Angkor in Cambodia.

타프롬

세월에 억눌린 장중한 타프롬
청록, 연노랑 외투입고
하늘 함께 떠받치는
번창하는 아틀라스 자식들에 붙잡힌 채

옛날 스님들 모여 경전 외웠지만
이젠 사람들 그 경치만 구경하려 가득하네
그 스님들 열정
눈요기 기쁨에 흐려지네

TA PROHM STEGOSAUR[67]

To a wall flock people and closely look
Into a bas-relief of a creature,
A boar or a Jurassic stegosaur,
Foliage as background or its own spines,
None without tail spikes or one mutated?
Never mind choosing one that pleases you.

[67] Photo taken on November 25, 2017, at Angkor in Cambodia.

156

타프롬 검룡

벽에 사람들이 몰려들어
자세히 들여다보네
생명체 부조를

멧돼지 인가 아니면 쥐라기 검룡인가?
배경이 나뭇잎 인가 아니면 등뼈인가?
꼬리 뿔이 없어서 아닌가
아니면 돌연변이 되었나?
괘념치 말고 그대 마음에 드는 걸 정하게나

ANGKOR WAT[68]

Soaring into the heavens like
Lotus buds, towers embody
Mount Meru for Hindu devas
And devis as Mount Olympus
For all Greek gods and goddesses,
Saved by a rectangular moat,
Three-nautical-mile Sea of Milk.
An epic carving says a myth
Where devas and asuras churn
Sea of Milk by Shiva's serpent
In Vishnu's aegis with Indra
Up and Kurma turtle below
To get dews for the immortal.
All pomp blurs in the mist of time;
Its demise is in mystery.
To be revealed is all fleeting.

---

[68] Photos on page 160 taken on November 25, 2017, at Angkor Wat in Cambodia.

앙코르와트

연꽃 봉오리처럼
하늘로 솟아오른 탑
힌두 신과 여신들 처소 메루산
그리스 신과 여신들의
올림푸스처럼 그려내고
세 해리가 넘는 우유 바다
해자로 지켰네

서사시적 조각
신화 이야기하네
신들과 아수라들
비슈누 후원에 시바의 뱀으로
우유 바다 휘저어
위로는 인드라
밑으로는 쿠르마 거북과 함께
불멸의 이슬 얻으려 한다는

모든 화려함은
시간 속에서 희미해지고
그 멸망은 비밀에 쌓여 있지만
모든 것 덧없음 드러날 것이네

Angkor Wat

Bas-relief of Churning of the ocean of milk in the Hindu
mythology at Angkor Wat

BAYON[69]

Smiles of compassion radiate
On leading faces of towers
Of sandstone jigsaw and lichened
Like Buddha or Bodhisattva
That Jayavarman longed to keep.

Victory Mount, Jayagiri
Named Banyan from the ambiance
Of Gautama's enlightenment
And called Bayon by the Khmer folk:
Genial smiles never mind the whim.

[69] Photo taken on November 25, 2017, at Angkor Thom in Cambodia.

바이욘

자비의 미소들 피어나네
여러 조각으로 된
이끼입은 사암의 탑 사면에서
자야바르만 바랬던 부처와 보살 같이

승리의 산, 자야기리
고타마 깨달음 장소의
나무에서 따온 반얀이라 불리우고
크메르인들 바이욘이라 하지만
온화한 미소 그 번덕
조금도 개의치 않네

FORBIDDEN CITY[70]

Behind the Meridian Gate,
Inner Golden Water Bridge lies
To Gate of Supreme Harmony.
For half the millennium of
The Great Ming and Qing Dynasties,
Untold mortals walked up the way,
And unceasing numbers follow
To the throne at the Museum,
The tablet at the Qianqing
Saying, "Let the righteous prevail."

[70] Photo taken on October 20, 2005, in Beijing, China.

자금성

오문 뒤에
내금수교 태화문으로 놓여있네
대명과 청 왕조 오백 년 동안
말로 다할 수 없는 사람들 그 길 걸었고
끊임없이 수 그 뒤따르네
고궁박물관의 왕좌로

건청궁 현판
대의가 널리 퍼지라 하니

GREAT WALL[71]

Ten-Thousand Li Long Wall, passing
Hills and valleys, meets Jiayu Pass
West and east, dips into Bo Sea
To defend against the Mongols
And the Machu without success.
The fall of the Qing Dynasty
Came not from the north but the south.

---

[71] Photo taken on October 19, 2005, in Beijing, China.

만리장성

만리장성
언덕, 계곡을 넘어
서쪽으로 가욕관 닿고
동쪽으로 발해에 담가
몽골과 만주족을 막으려 했지만
실패로 끝나버린
청나라의 몰락은
북쪽 아닌 남쪽에서 왔구나.

TAJ MAHAL[72]

Sha Jahan's love for his consort,
Mumtaz Mahal, raised Taj Mahal
In white marble of symmetry
For excessive expense and time,
Spellbinding viewers without fail;
His confinement at Agra Fort
Soothed in looking at Taj Mahal
Time and again from Muthamman
And pining for his changeless love
To rest together with her there.

---

[72] Photo taken on July 12, 2017, in Agra, India.

타지마할

배우자 뭄타즈 마할에 대한
샤자한의 사랑
과도한 비용과 시간 들여
대칭의 흰 대리석 타지마할 세워
어김없이 보는 사람 매료하네

아그라 포트 그의 유폐 삶
무타만에서 타지마할 자주 바라보며
자신의 변함없는 사랑 달랬네
그곳 그녀와 함께 잠들길
애타게 그리며

MANIKARNIKA GHAT[73]

Awakening at dawn was a boat ride,
Starting from Dashashwamedah upstream
To Assi, downstream to Malviya Bridge,
And ending at Manikarnika Ghat;
Baba Mashan Nath Temple watched the fire
On the Ghat with ironwood stored for pyres.
A mourner in a white robe with his head
Shaven was at the end of cremation;
He took a clay pot with Ganga water,
Faced away from the fire, and smashed the pot
By tossing it backward from his shoulder.
To free the soul is to break with the earth!

[73] Photo taken on July 14, 2017, on the Ganges.

마니카르니카 가트

새벽 자각은 갠지스강 보트 여정,
다시시와메드에서 시작하여 하류 아씨,
상류 말비야 다리,
마니카르니카 가트로 끝나는

바바마산나트 사원
화장 장작더미 아이언우드 쌓아 놓은
가트의 불 지켜보았네

흰 옷 두른 삭발한 상주의 화장 마무리,
갠지스강물 담은 옹기 들고
불 등지고 어깨에서
그 옹기 뒤로 던져 깨트렸네.

영혼을 자유롭게 하는 건
세속과 인연 끊는 것이라네!

SHIVA OF ELEPHANTA[74]

Two halves are Shiva in Elephanta;
One half is full bosomed, not the other.
Lithe Parvati and Shiva with Nandi
Close eyes to meditate for composure.
Duality is Shiva's attribute:
Marriage of mercy and ferocity;
The union of the halved leads to oneness.

---

[74] Photo taken on January 5, 2018, in Elephanta Island near Mumbai, India.

엘레판타 시바

두 반 조각인 엘레판타 시바
한 반쪽은 풍만한 가슴,
다른 반쪽엔 없어
나긋나긋한 파르바티,
난디와 함께한 시바
눈 지극히 감고
평온을 명상하네
이중성은 시바의 특성
자비와 사나움의 융합
나누어진 반 조각
결합으로 하나되네

ENIGMA OF DONA PAULA[75]

A romantic tale an Indian told
Stirred me to head to Goa for its trace:
Dona Paula, the viceroy's daughter
Who fell in love with a poor fisherman;
Their banned love led her to jump off a cliff.
In the other version, her husband went
Fishing and never returned; waiting for
Him perpetually, she turned to stone.
In fact, she came to Goa, wedded to
Dom Antonio Souto Maior, and
Worked long for bettering villagers' lives,
And the village was renamed after her.
The riddle unveiled leaves dismay and calm.

---

[75] Photo taken on January 6, 2018, at Dona Paula of Goa, India.

도나 폴라 수수께끼

인도인이 말한 낭만적인 이야기
날 자극하여 그 흔적 찾으려
고아로 가게 했네
도나 폴라, 총독의 딸
가난한 어부와 사랑에 빠졌지만
그 금지된 사랑으로
그녀 절벽에서 뛰어내렸다는

고기를 잡으려 갔다
돌아오지 않는 남편
끝없이 기다리다 돌이 되었다는
변형된 이야기

돔 안토니오 소우토 마이오르와
결혼한 후 고아에 와
그곳 마을 사람들의 복지에 오랫동안 힘쓰다
그곳 그녀 이름 따라 부르게 되었다는 사실

밝혀진 수수께끼에 당황과 평온만이

HAMPI[76]

Aqueducts and Pushkarani,
Tiered water tank for rituals
Effuse the charm of consonance.
Lotus Mahal, enriched with domes
Of mesmerizing ambience
And Elephant's Stable unscathed,
Reveal the prosperity of
Empire Vijayanaraga.
Mahanavami, Queen's Bath, Fort . . .
Two centuries' feat was ravaged
From Muslim pillage of six months,
Unfolded forlorn in ruins;
Lamenting all is vanity.

---
[76] Photo taken on January 8, 2018, at Pushkarani of Hampi in India.

함피

수로와
의식을 위한 다섯 층계 수조,
푸쉬카라니
조화의 매력 발산하고
매혹적인 분위기 돔
가득한 연꽃궁전과
손상되지 않은 코끼리 우리
비자야나가라 왕국의 번영 드러내네

마하나바미, 여왕의 목욕탕, 성채...
이백 년 위업
어싯 달 동안 회교도 약탈로
황량하게 폐허 드러내며
슬퍼하네
모든 것 헛되다고

VITTALA TEMPLE[77]

Stone chariot for Garuda
Of Vishnu spellbinds the gazer
Entering Vittala Temple.
Pillars of Mandapam as tapped
Sing their tunes—Sa, Re, Ga, and Ma;
Hearers become her captives as
Odysseus, Calypso held.

[77] Photo taken on January 8, 2018, at Vittala Temple of Hampi in India.

비탈라 사원

비슈누의 가루다 위한
돌 전차
비탈라 사원 찾아와 보는 이 빠져들고
만다팜 기둥 똑똑 두드리면
제 음조 사레가마 노래하고
듣는 이 그녀 포로 되네
칼립소에 붙잡힌 오디세우스처럼

THE SCREW PINE[78]

A firm screw pine encircles rock
With roots in fetters tied on it,
As tethered like Prometheus.
Palpable is the steadfast cry
"I will be free to walk away."

<hr />

[78] Photo taken on January 20, 2018, in Chennai, India.

판다누스

판다누스 한 그루
사슬에 매인 프로메테우스처럼
바위에 묶인 뿌리로 바위를 감싸네

느낄 수 있는 그 확고한 외침
"내 자유로이 걸어 나갈 거야."

MATHO MONASTERY[79]

Matho Monastery near Leh,
Bustling with throngs of devotees,
Young and old, pupils and laymen
For Dalai Lama from the morn;
Mandala drawn white on the ground,
The green carpet unfolded and
Petals strewn with spirit lifted.
Matho brightened in his sermon;
The stepped petals gleaned as blessings.

[79] Photo taken on July 20, 2017, at Matho Monastery near Leh in Ladakh, India.

마토 사원

레 가까이 마토 사원
신심이 깊은 사람들
젊거나 나이든 이,
학생들과 일반인들로
분주하여라
아침부터 달라이라마 위하여

바닥에 만다라
하얗게 그려 놓고
녹색 카펫 펼쳐
고양된 정신으로 꽃잎 뿌려
그의 설법 마토 밝히고
그가 지나간 꽃잎
축복으로 모아 담기네

LADAKH[80]

The cyan Pangong Tso nestles
Coyly in the Himalayas,
Wreathed with wild roses in full bloom;
Near them, the primordial scent
Soaks body and soul with delight.
The Ladaki become nature,
Erasing greed and envy and
Turning the wretched to the blithe.

---

80 Photo taken on July 21, 2017, at Pangong Tso in Ladakh, India.

라닥

청록의 판공초
히말라야에 수줍게 자리잡고
활짝 핀 야생 장미 화환 둘러
그 가까이 가면 원시의 향기
몸과 마음 기쁨으로 적시네

라닥 사람들 자연이 되어
탐욕과 시기 지우고
가없음 쾌활함으로 바꾸네

KIYOMIZUDERA TEMPLE[81]

Pure waters from Otowa Falls
Dividing into three conduits:
Long life, success at school, and love
As each boon to their imbibers
Test their modesty to drink one.
After the test, the wooden stage
Shows the unsung side of the world.

---

[81] Photo taken on June 20, 2011 in Kyoto, Japan.

청수사

오토와 폭포의 맑은 물
세 도관으로 나누어져
장수, 학업 성취 그리고 사랑을
각각의 혜택으로
마시는 사람에게 주며
하나만 마시는
그들의 소박함 시험하네
시험 뒤 그 나무 무대
세상의 알지 못한 면 보여주네

KINKAKUJI[82]

A golden pavilion unfolds
On a pond with pine trees and rocks
In two upper floors in gold leaf
And the lower in white plaster,
Decked with a phoenix on the roof;
The shogun's retreat became Zen
Temple with lavishness, burnt thrice
And rebuilt with the innate grace.

[82] Photo taken on June 20, 2011, in Kyoto, Japan.

금각사

금색 정자
송암으로 된 연못에
위 두 층은 금박으로
아래층은 하얀 회반죽으로 되어
지붕 봉황으로 꾸며
펼쳐지네

쇼군의 은퇴처
호화로움 갖는
선종 사찰되어
세번의 소실로
본래의 우아함으로
다시 지어졌네

KUANG SI FALLS[83]

Mist wafts amid a multitiered waterfall;
Her silvery hands knead craggy rocks
Gently to a crafted garden,
Veiled with pearls.

She whispers a sweet lullaby in lush foliage,
Disrobing white silk dress
To innate jade green;
Irresistible to plunge into her.

---

[83] Photo taken on November 4, 2017, in Luang Prabang, Laos.

쾅 시 폭포

물안개
여러 층의 폭포 감돌고
그녀 은빛 손으로
울퉁불퉁한 기암
부드럽게 반죽하여
정원 만들어
진주로 가려 놓네

무성한 잎새사이로
달콤한 자장가 속삭이며
히얀 비단옷 벗고
본래 비취옥 드러내면
그녀에 뛰어들고 싶음
억제할 수 없네

TAK BAT AT LUANG PRABANG[84]

In the mist 'fore the sunrise, Lao women
In scarfs kneeling on mats, with small baskets
Of sticky rice and bags of diverse snacks,
Waiting for barefoot monks in saffron robes
Earnestly to donate the offering
And earn spiritual lift in return
To sense avarice tapering away.
Trains of monks, old and young, from near temples
Walking in the seniority aglow
On footpath in tacit meditation,
Carrying the lidded bowls, allowing
A scoop of rice or other from each one
Eagerly to let merits piled for them
And turn the place filled with royal Buddhas.

[84] Photo taken on November 5, 2017, in Luang Prabang, Laos.

루앙푸라방 탁발

동트기 전 안개 속
라오 아낙네
스카프 감고 매트에 무릎 꿇고
작은 바구니에 달라붙는 쌀 담고
여러가지 과자봉지 가지고
담황색 승복 걸친
맨발의 스님을 기다리며
지성으로 공물을 바치고
보답으로 정신적 고양 얻어
탐욕 점차 작아지게

가까운 절 스님들의 행렬
나이 들고 젊은 스님
출가 순으로 줄지어 환하게
묵언의 명상 속에서 길 밝히며
옆에 걸친 뚜껑 덮은 바리대에 허용하는 것
각 보시자의 밥 한 수저나 과자 한 봉지
열렬히 그들 위해 공덕 쌓아
고귀한 부처로 그 곳 가득 채우려

DOK CHAMPA[85]

Dok champa,
Thy lustrous white tinges with canary
In the middle and amber in the core;
At morn, thou greet a Laotian damsel
And alight on her ebony tresses;
She is a temple, fragrant and divine.
Not a soul can resist thy adornment.
What a magic of thy sincerity!
O dok champa.

[85] Photo taken on November 5, 2017, in Luang Prabang, Laos.

독 참파

독 참파
그대 윤기도는 흰색 물들어
중간엔 샛노랗고
한가운덴 황갈색
아침 라오스 처녀 맞이하여
그녀의 칠흑 같은 머리칼 위 내려앉아
그녀는 사원이네
향기롭고 거룩한
그대의 장식 거절할 이 없지
그대 순수함의 마법이여!
오 독 참파여

THE PHEWA BATHER[86]

She arches her supple body,
Dips her long hair into Phewa,
And looks at ripples before her.

Annapurna south, Fishtail and
More Annapurna, side by side—
All are immersed into the lake.

In her lush tresses is the boon.

[86] Photo taken on January 9, 2011, in Pokhara, Nepal.

페와의 머리 감는 여자

나긋나긋한 허리를 굽여
긴 머리 페와에 담가내고
그녀 앞 작은 파문 응시하네

안나푸르나 사우스, 피쉬테일,
안나푸르나 준봉들 나란히
모두 페와에 잠겼네

그녀 풍성한 심딘같은 머리엔
그 은혜

MAYA DEVI TEMPLE[87]

Quietude adorns the temple with mist;
Next to it stands the Ashoka pillar,
Protected by iron grill in gold leaf.
Unsung lie ruins of monasteries
Along with stupas and the tiered square pond,
Where Maya Devi took a bath before
Giving birth to Siddhartha Gautama,
And an age-old bodhi tree embellished
With numerous prayer flags in color.
In progress is excavating structures
Ranging from the third century BC
To the seventh century AD inside;
At a corner settles the Marker stone,
The Birthplace of Shakyamuni Buddha,
As a seal of enlightenment for man.

87 Photo taken on January 10, 2011, at Maya Devi Temple in Lumbini, Nepal.

마야 데비 사원

평온함 사원 안개로 꾸미고
사원 옆 아소카 기둥
금박 입은 철창에 둘려 쌓여
사원 폐허 알려지지 않은 채
불탑,
고타마 낳기 전
마하 데비 목욕했던
층계로 된 사각 못
그리고 수많은 다양한 색깔
기도 깃발 장식한
오래 세월 거친
보리수와 함께 있네.
내부에서 기원전 3세기에서
서기 7세기까지의 구조물
발굴 이루어지고
한 구석엔 석가모니 부처
탄생자리 표지석
인류 위한 깨달음 증표로
놓여있네.

PASHUPATINATH PYRES[88]

Yellow garlands cover three layers of
Logs on a dais for a corpse dipped thrice
In the Bagmati flowing to Ganges.
Tens of bodies are burning in a day;
Billowing smokes spread over the temple,
Filling air with the stench of burning flesh;
The process is watched on the other side.
All the valued lose their magic in there;
The jarring smell goads me to leave the place.

[88] Photo taken on January 12, 2011, at Pashupatinath Temple in Kathmandu, Nepal.

파슈파티나트 장작더미

단상의 삼 층으로 쌓은 장작더미
노란 화환으로 덮여
갠지스강으로 흘러가는 바그마티에
세차례 적신 시신 기다린다

단 하루 수십 시신 화장되어
솟아오르는 검은 연기 사원 뒤덮고
살 타는 역한 냄새 공기를 채우고
건너편에서 그 과정 지켜본다

값진 모든 것 그 곳에서 마력을 잃고
거슬리는 냄새에 자리를 뜬다

SIGIRIA[89]

Vestiges of palaces linger
In lilies of a boulder pond
On the top of the massive rock.
Lively frescoes color the rock,
And a damsel in cloud strewing
Petals portends you're in Heaven.
The mirror wall conveys verses
Fraught with age-old worldly feelings.

[89] Photo taken on January 24, 2018, at Sigiria Rock in Sri Lanka.

시기리아

왕궁의 흔적
거대한 바위 꼭대기
바위 연못 수련에
어른거리네

생기에 넘친 프레스코 그림들
바위를 채색하고
구름 속 선녀
꽃잎 흩날리며
그 곳 선계라 알리네

오랜 세상 느낌
가득한 이야기
거울 벽 전해주네

V. AUSTRALIA

KOALA[90]

Are you dozing
On a eucalypt branch, leaning
With all limbs dangling?

Are you acting
To smiles and calm, kindling
Even souls in anguish and suffering?

You are an angel in gray clothing
without flying.

90 Photo taken on December 3, 2017, at Paradise Country in Australia.

코알라

너 졸고 있니?
유칼립투스 가지에 기대어
사지를 늘어뜨린 채

너 연기하고 있니?
온갖 고통에 찌들어 있는 영혼에조차
미소와 평온 주려고

너는 분명 잿빛 옷 입은 천사
날지 않는

POKAREKARE ANNA[91]

In Rotorua was young Hinemoa,
Chief's daughter; on Mokoia Island
Of Rotorua was Tutanekai,
Bastard son of another tribal chief.
At a meeting of tribes, their encounter
Turned to love, forbidden by his status.
Night after night, Hinemoa rowed to him;
Her family beached all the canoes up.
On the lakeside fidgeted Hinemoa,
Plaintive and despondent over the date.
On the isle Tutanekai pined for her,
Fluting; the tunes wafting across the lake
Inflamed her to swim only with six gourds
Fastened to her for their happy union.
Pokarekare Ana!

---

[91] Photo taken on December 12, 2017, in Rotorua, New Zealand.

포카레카레 아나

로토루아에 있었지
족장의 딸 히네모아
로토루아 모코이아 섬에 있었지
다른 족장의 사생아 투타네카이
부족들의 모임에서
두 사람 만나 사랑하게 되었지
금단의 사랑, 그의 출생이력으로

밤마다 히네모아 노 저어 그 찾아가기에
그녀 가족 모든 카누 땅 위에 올려놓았지
호숫가 히네모아 만남 애태웠지
애처롭게 낙담한 채,
섬에서 투타네카이 피리 불렀지
그녀 갈망하며
호수 건너온 그 피리소리
그녀 불 붙였네
몸에 여섯 개 표주박만 묶고
헤엄쳐가 얻은 그들의 행복한 결혼
포카레카레 아나!

209

FIJIAN CHRISTMAS TREES[92]

Flame trees replace Christmas trees in Fiji,
Blooming in November to all, scarlet
In yuletide, adorned with rooster flowers.
Its nostalgic name is from children's play.
Taking stamens out from a flower bud,
Boys hook a stamen head up another
And pull theirs; the boy with its head intact
Wins the duel, and the play continues
Till all stamens are used. Its pistil is
A crown for the last triumphant winner.
Verdure mingled with blossom and the blue.

---

[92] Photo taken on December 14, 2017, at Port Denarau in Fiji.

피지 크리스마스트리

피지 크리스마스트리는 불꽃나무
십일월 꽃이 피어 진홍색으로
성탄절 장식하는 수탉 꽃

그 향수 젖은 이름
아이들의 놀이에서 오네
꽃봉오리에서 수술 꺼내
두 수술머리를 서로 걸어 잡아당겨
머리가 달린 아이 이기고
수술머리 다 할 때까지 겨루어
최종 승자 왕관은 암술머리가 되는

푸르름
꽃, 하늘과 어우러지네

TIVUA ISLET[93]

A white-rimmed sombrero floating
Between Neptune and the heavens,
Welcomes with stretched arms arrivals
Of the blithe sail from Denarau
On Spirit of the Pacific:
Tivua, utopia for
Bathing with a breeze at a hut.

---

[93] Photo taken on December 14, 2017, in Tivua Island in Fiji.

티부아 섬

하얀 차양 두른 모자
바다와 구름 드리운 하늘 사이에 떠
태평양 스피리트 타고 즐겁게
데나라우에서 온 손님들
팔 펼쳐 맞이하는
티부아,
유토피아
오두막에서
산들바람으로 씻기에

VI. EUROPE

MERRY-GO-ROUND[94]

Fragrance near Sacré Cœur,
From a dainty angel
Mounting a snow-white horse
Poseidon used to ride
On a merry-go-round,
Suffusing Montmartre's vale,

Effulgence covering
The whole merry-go-round,
Coming from the angel
With an engaging smile
As Mother does on Child,
Lighting the Universe.

[94] Composed on December 8, 2016. Illustration based on a photo taken in January 1990 in Paris, France.

회전목마

사크레 쾨르 가까이 향내음
회전목마 위
포세이돈 곧잘 타던 눈처럼 하얀 말 탄
앙증맞은 천사에게 나와
몽마르트르 골 퍼져 나가네

회전목마 온통 덮은
눈부신 광휘,
성모 예수에게 하듯
매력적인 미소 띤
그 천사에게 나와
우주 밝혀 주네

REMINISCENCE OF OVERSTRAND[95]

On River Mersey Overstrand
Held the two-story house in bricks.
On the wall of the snug backyard
Clung small English Cox apple trees
With sweet and savory apples.
In furrows at the backyard grew
Leeks and carrots hedged with laurels,
A rosemary behind the gate
Filling with newly budded leaves.

[95] Photo taken on June 16, 2014, at Cressington Esplanade in Liverpool, England.

오버스트랜드 추억

머지 강가 오버스트랜드
벽돌 이층집 있었지
아늑한 뒷마당 담
달콤하고 맛있는 사과 달린
작은 잉글랜드 칼스 나무 달라붙어 있고
월계수 울타리 쳐진 뒷마당 이랑
부추와 당근 자라고
문 뒤 로즈메리
새로 싹튼 잎들 가득했시

SALZBURG[96]

Hohensalzburg Castle, perched on
Festungsberg, resonates with tunes
Of Salzburg from Mozart's birthplace,
Vibrant as in Die Zauberflöte,
Carefree as Papageno, and
Demanding as Queen of the Night.
To fairyland looms a wormhole.

[96] Photo taken on November 5, 2010, in Salzburg, Austria.

잘츠부르크

호헨잘츠부르크 성
페스퉁스베르그 언덕에 걸터앉아
모짜르트 탄생지로부터
잘츠부르크 선율과 공명하며
마술피리에서처럼 생기 넘치네
파파게노처럼 태평하고
밤의 여왕처럼 많을 걸 요구하며.
요정의 나라로 웜홀 드러나네
어렴풋이

MOZART GRAVE[97]

In Wiener Zentralfriedhof
Rest Beethoven, Schubert, Brahms, Strauss . . .
With Ludwig Boltzmann, deviser
Of entropy for disorder,
And stands Mozart's memorial.
Contented with Enlightenment,
Mozart, with the Mourning Genius
Leaning on a broken column,
Rests at St Marxer Friedhof.

---

[97] Photo taken on October 31, 2010, at St. Marxer Friedhof in Vienna, Austria.

모짜르트 묘

비엔나 중앙 묘지에
베토벤, 슈베르트, 브람스, 슈트라우스…
무질서에 대한 엔트로피 고안한
루트비히 볼츠만 함께 잠들어 있고
모짜르트 기념비 서있네

계몽주의 만족했던
모짜르트 잠들어 있네
부서진 기둥에 기대 챈
슬퍼하는 수호신과 함께
성 마르크스 묘지에

PRAGUE[98]

Prague Castle with River Vltava
Unfolds mesmerizing beauty,
As prophesied the young princess
Libuše, the founder of Prague;
A cityscape adorned with spires
Satiates the Powder Tower.

[98] Photo taken on November 3, 2010, in Prague, Czech Republic.

프라하

프라하 성 블타바 강과
매혹적인 아름다움 펼치네
젊은 공주
프라하를 만든 리부세 예언했듯
첨탑으로 꾸며진 도시 경관
파우더 탑에 부족함 없네

KARLOVY VARY[99]

The scenic setting with hot springs,
Comforting, draws admiration,
Unfeigned even in the first call,
Named Carlsbad after Charles IV.

Goethe and Beethoven sauntered.
Chopin stayed there with his parents.
Turgenev made several calls.

Chilly climate can be soothing
With hot springs and Becherovka.

---

[99] Photo taken on November 3, 2010, in Karlovy Vary, Czech Republic.

카를로비 바리

그림같은 배경 편안케 하는 온천
첫 만남에서도 꾸밈없는 찬사 끌어내며
찰스 4세 이름 따라 칼스바드라 불리네

괴테와 베토벤 거닐었고
쇼팽 부모와 함께 보냈고
투르게네프 여러 차례 방문했다네

차가운 기후도
온천과 베체로브카도
마음 진정시킬 수 있네

THE LITTLE MERMAID[100]

The lithe mermaid in bronze, sitting
On a rock at Langelinie,
Downcast, ponders on the harm done.
The wish to have a human soul
Was damnable with the head sawn—
The base blasted or marks defaced?
The taut Valkyrie on horseback
In Churchill Park runs to battles
To choose the slain for Valhalla,
Roaring, "Fear not death! Live in praise!"

---

[100] Photos on page 230 taken on May 13, 2014, in Copenhagen, Denmark.

인어공주

나긋나긋한 청동 인어
랑엘리니 바위에 앉아 눈을 내리깔고
지난 모든 상처 곰곰이 생각하네
사람 되고자 하는 바람,
목이 잘리거나
앉은 자리가 폭파당하거나
외관이 손상당한 자국으로
비난해야 했는가?

처칠공원
팽팽하게 긴장한 말 탄 발키리
전쟁터로 달려가네
발할라 위한 죽은 자 선택하려
"두려워 마라 죽음을! 찬미속에서 살라!"
포효하며

Statue of the Little Mermaid at Langelinie in Copenhagen, Denmark

Statue of a Valkyrie at Churchill Park in Copenhagen, Denmark

SHAKESPEARE[101]

Stratford-upon-Avon nestles
On the River Avon, shining
With the place of birth and demise
Of the timeless poet quoted,
Buried at Holy Trinity
Humoring, "GOOD FREND FOR jESVS
SAKE FORBEARE, TO DIGG THE DVST . . . BONES."
Let him rest with his family.

[101] Photo taken on June 9, 2014, at the Holy Trinity Church in Stratford-upon-Avon, England.

셰익스피어

에이븐 강가
시간 초월한 인용되는 시인
태어나고 죽음 맞이한
스트랫퍼더폰에이븐 빛나네

홀리 트리니티에 묻혀서도
해학적으로 말하네
"좋은 친구여, 제발 흙 파지 말게나...뼈를..."
그를 가족과 함께 쉬게 하소서

STONEHENGE[102]

On the grassland stand sarsen stones
And bluestone in a ring apart,
With the Heelstone at its entrance;
Moved afar from Preseli Hills
Millennia ago, bluestones
Served burial or ritual,
Unavoidable from the birth.
Facing triliths sits a damsel
With her eyes closed; a ritual
Starts the spiritual journey.

---

[102] Photo taken on June 10, 2014, in Wiltshire, England.

스톤헨지

초원에 대사암과 청석
입구 힐스톤과 떨어져
둥글게 서있네

저 멀리 프레슬리 힐스에서
수천년 전 옮겨온 청석들
태어나서 피할 수 없는
매장과 의식 위해서

삼석탑 바라보며
한 처녀 눈 감고 앉자
정신적 여정의 의식 시작되네

TALLINN TOWN HALL[103]

Lofty corpus in gray limestone,
Slanting roofs in red clay tiles, and
Octahedral tower decked with
A spire of the Old Thomas vane
Shape into the Tallinn Town Hall,
Peculiar and independent,
Revealing her diverse functions,
Parapet and council meeting.

---

[103] Photo taken on May 7, 2014, in Tallinn, Estonia.

탈린 시청

회색 석회암 몸체
붉은 진흙 타일의 경사진 지붕
올드 토마스 바람개비 첨탑 가진 팔각 탑
탈린 시청
독특하고 독자적인 모습 만드네,
자신의 다양한 역할
방어벽과 의원회의 드러내며

FINLANDIA[104]

Passio Musicae, made of
Undulating pipes, accounts for
Sibelius Finlandia,
Wakening Finland to be freed
From the yoke of Russian Empire
With thunderous ensemble of
Trombones, French horns, and timpani,
Signaling a new day dawning,
Thy mission completed in full.

[104] Photo taken on May 4, 2014, at the Sibelius Park in Helsinki, Finland.

핀란디아

물결치는 듯한 파이프로 된 열정적 음악
시벨리우스 핀란디아 말하네
새로운 날 옴 알리는
트롬본, 혼, 팀파니
우레같은 합주로
러시아 제국의 멍에에서
자유로워지라
핀란드 깨우는
그대의 사명 온전히 다했네

PROVINS[105]

A medieval nostalgia
Permeates into Provins through
Ramparts, Tour César, St. Quiriace,
And Tithe Barn with rooms and cellars,
For Champagne fairs in its heyday
And a shelter to denizens.
A rill embellished with flowers
Adds its seamless charm to the town.

[105] Photo taken on September 12, 2010, in Provins, France.

240

프로뱅

중세 그리움 프로뱅
성벽, 시저 타워, 생퀴리아스,
방과 저장실로
전성기에 샹파느 장과
주민들의 비난처로 쓰였던
십일조 창고에 스며 있네
꽃으로 단장한 시내
끊김 없는 매력 도시에 더하네

MONT-SAINT-MICHEL[106]

At neap tides arise flats with marsh;
Mainland unites Mont-Saint-Michel.
Fortress in an isle at spring tides,
Invincible and unyielding,
During the Hundred Years' War
Embodied the Jeanne d'Arc, raising
A torch to free France from England
Like Saint Michael atop the spire.

---
[106] Photo taken on June 6, 2014, at Mont-Saint-Michel in France.

몽생미셸

조금엔 모래톱과 습지 드러내어
대륙과 만나는 몽생미셸
한사리땐 섬의 성채가 되네
정복당하지도 굽히지도 않는,
백년전쟁 동안
그 잔 다르크로 구현되어
첨탑 위 성 미카엘처럼
횃불 들어올려
영국으로부터 프랑스 해방시켰네

PHILOSOPHENWEG[107]

Strolling on Philosophenweg
Across the Neckar from the Schloss
Brings back names, thoughts, and an epic,
Critique of Pure Reason of Kant,
Hegel's dialectic logic,
And the Song of the Nibelungs.

Kriemhild's tragic love for Siegfried
Turned to the atrocious revenge,
Decapitating her brother
And destroying herself. Alas!

107 Photo taken on September 24, 2008, in Heidelberg, Germany.

철학자의 길

성에서 네카어 강 건너
철학자의 길 걸으니
이름, 사상 그리고 한 서사시
떠오른다
칸트 순수이성비판,
헤겔 변증법적 논리,
니벨룽겐의 노래

지크프리트에 대한
크림힐트 비극적 사랑
잔혹한 복수가 되어
오빠의 목 베고
자신도 파멸하게 되었으니
아아!

BRANDENBURG GATE[108]

Victoria on Quadriga
On the top of Brandenburg Gate
Saw the rise and fall of the Wall,
Dividing Berlin into two
For twenty-eight years, taking lives,
And voices peace and unity;
The Korean Peninsula,
Divided into south and north
By the DMZ, wide and long,
For long three scores or more of years,
Will see the fall to unity?

---

[108] Photo taken on May 19, 2014, in Berlin, Germany.

브란덴부르크 문

4두2륜 전차 탄 빅토리아
브란덴부르크 문위에서
장벽 세워지고 무너지는 걸 보았지
베를린 둘로 28년간 나누어
수백명 목숨 희생시킨,
이제 평화와 통일 말하네

넓고도 긴 그 DMZ로
기나긴 60년이상 동안
남과 북으로 분단된,
한반도
그 무너짐으로 통일을 볼 것인가?

GIBRALTAR[109]

On a pillar of Hercules'
Reclines the Rock with the castle,
Gazing Africa o'er the Strait.
In St. Michael's cave of limestone,
Cloaked with varied stalactites
For events, waits Cathedral Cave.
The Ibrahim-al-Ibrahim
At Europa Point longs for God.

[109] Photo taken on September 23, 2010, in Gibraltar.

지브롤터

헤라클레스 기둥 위에
지브롤터와 성 누워서
해협 건너 아프리카 바라보네

다채로운 종유석으로 치장한
석회석 성 마이클 동굴의 성당 동굴
행사를 기다리네

이브라힘안이브라힘
유로파 포인트에서 신을 갈망하는데

ACROPOLIS[110]

Parthenon and Erechtheion,
With Athena Nike Temple,
Gated by the Propylaea,
Amass in the Acropolis,
Erected on a rock outcrop;
The theater of Dionysus,
Facing the polis, manifests
Its past cultural opulence
For seventeen thousand viewers.
Advent of Socrates, destined!

---

[110] Photo taken on May 30, 2014, in Athens, Greece.

아크로폴리스

파르테논, 에레크테이온
아테네 니케 템플, 문 달고
드러난 바위에 세워져
아크로폴리스에 모여 있네.

디오니소스 극장
아크로폴리스 바라보며
17,000 명의 관객 위한
과거 문화의 풍요함 분명히 드러내네.

소크라테스의 출현, 예정된!

SANTORINI[111]

A hot spring bubbling in the blue
Without concealing her passion
Beckons intrepid souls on ships
To swim into her like Circe,
Enthralled for a day unless calls.

Blue and white mount terra cotta,
Arousing Greek mythical tinge.
Paths at Oia bustle with crowds
For sunsets fair or overcast,
Pleasing all without exceptions.

[111] Photo taken on June 2, 2014, in Santorini, Greece.

252

산토리니

바다에서 샘솟는 온천
자신의 열정 드러내며
선상의 용감한 사람들
자기에게 헤엄쳐 오라
키르케처럼 손짓하네
부르는 소리 없다면
온종일 마음 빼앗긴 채

적갈색위에 파랑, 하양
그리스 신화 느낌 일으키며
오이아 작은 길
사람들로 붐비네.
맑거나 흐리거나
예외없이 모두에게
기쁨주는 일몰 보러

BUDAPEST[112]

Országház, facing the Danube River,
Stands in contrasting red and white,
Characterizing Budapest.
Before the House are sundry shoes
On the river without owners,
Three thousand or more, with the Jews
Shot by Arrow Cross militia
And fallen into the Danube.

[112] Photo taken on October 28, 2010, in Budapest, Hungary.

부다페스트

오르사가츠
다뉴브강 바라보며
빨강, 하양으로 대비된
부다페스트 특색 드러내네.
의회 앞 강변엔
주인 잃은 잡다한 신발들
유대인들 포함하여 삼천이상
애로우 크로스 민병대의 총 맞아
다뉴브 속으로 떨어진 이들

COLOSSEUM[113]

A giant amphitheater
Lies with the arena used for
Animal hunts, bloody contests
Of gladiators and pastime,
Underground hypogeum for
Animals and gladiators,
Special box for the Emperor,
Podium for the senators,
And tiers defined for their status,
The grave cross of the podium
Lighting the follies with wisdom.

[113] Photo taken on October 2, 2009, in Rome, Italy.

콜로세움

거대한 원형경기장
동물 사냥, 피투성이의 검투사 경기,
오락을 위한 아레나,
동물과 검투사의 지하실,
황제를 위한 특별 연단,
원로원 위원들을 위한 연단과
직위 따라 정해진 층계들로 되어있고
연단 엄숙한 십자가
그 어리석음 지혜로 밝혀주네

VENICE[114]

Two patron saints of Venezia,
San Marco and Teodoro,
On a pair of granite columns,
Regard Piazza San Marco.

From the Constantinople spoils,
A lion and two angel's wings
Turned to San Macro and fragments
Fitted to San Teodoro?

베니스

베네치아 두 수호신,
산 마르코, 산 테오도로
한 쌍 화강암 기둥위에 서서
산 마르코 광장 응시하네.

콘스탄티노플 전리품,
사자와 천사의 양 날개
산 마르코되고
부서진 조각들
산 테오도로로 맞췄나?

TRUE REWARD[115]

Chance encounter at Akershus:
Harald V in A·2 flying
The Royal Standard, the gold-crowned
Lion with an axe of white blade
On a red flag, waved with a smile
To me, waving by the roadside.

Lovely phrase in the Palace Square:
At the statue of King Charles John,
His conviction is still living:
"FOLKETS KJÆRLIGHET MIN BELÖNNING."
The love of people, my reward,
Could save wrongdoing of rulers.

---
[115] Photo taken on May 13, 2014, in Oslo, Norway.

진정한 보상

아커서스성의 우연한 만남,
붉은 색 바탕
은도끼 든 금관 쓴 사자 왕기
휘날리는 A·2의 하랄드 5세
웃음으로 손 흔들어 주네
손 흔드는 길가 나에게

왕궁 광장의 아름다운 구절,
찰스 존 국왕 동상에
그의 신념 여전히 살아있네
민중의 사랑 나의 보상
민중의 사랑, 나의 보상이면
통치자의 비행 면할 수 있을 터인데

261

AUSCHWITZ[116]

"ARBEIT MACHT FREI," dancing in black,
Hangs above an iron portal
After a gate in black and white;
An electric barbed wire fence braced
By concrete poles chokes the free air.

Enmity is acquired or not?
Animosity is subdued
By compassion or past lessons?

---

[116] Photo taken on April 23, 2014, in Auschwitz, Poland.

아우슈비츠

"일이 너를 자유롭게 하리라"
검게 춤추듯
흑백 차단기 뒤
철 정문위에 걸려있고
콘크리트 기둥에 걸쳐진
전기 가시철망 담장
자유로운 공기 질식케 하네.

증오 후천적인가 아닌가?
증오 사랑이나 옛 교훈으로 극복되나?

ST. MARY'S BASILICA[117]

The Gothic St. Mary's Altar
In a triptych carved in linden,
Death and Assumption of Mary
Centered with the Twelve Apostles,
Moved to Germany and back home,
A Polish national treasure;
A broken note of a trumpet
Is hourly heard from the tower,
Reminding the trumpeter shot
In his throat while sounding the raid.

[117] Photo taken on April 24, 2014, in Krakow, Poland.

성모 마리아 성당

성모 마리아의 고딕 양식 제단,
보리수에 새겨진 삼연작
가운데 성모 죽음과 몽소승천
열두제자와 함께,
독일로 옮겨졌다 집으로 돌아온
폴란드 국보

끊긴 트럼펫 연주
매시간 마다 성당 탑에서 들리지
침략 알리다 목에 화살 맞은
나팔수 기리는

INÊS DE CASTRO[118]

Destiny of the fervid love,
Led to wedlock in secrecy,
And death in the merciless ruse
Of her groom's father Alfonso,
Born to a coronation tale,
Lauding that love transcended death.
RIP at Alcobaça,
Together 'til the Judgment Day
To rise from their marble coffins
And face each other with the love.

---

[118] Photo taken on October 5, 2010, at Alcobaça Monastery in Portugal.

이네스 데 까스트로

그 불같은 사랑의 운명
남몰래 맺어져
신랑아버지 알폰소의
무자비한 계략에 죽음 맞이했고,
대관식 이야기로 살아나
사랑 죽음도 초월한다 칭송 받네.

알코바사 수도원에
함께 최후 심판의 날까지 잠들다
내리석 무덤에서 일어나
그 사랑으로 서로 마주 보려고

RED SQUARE[119]

Observing the siege of Kazan
With flames rising into the sky,
Saint Basil's Cathedral stands glad,
Suggesting Heavenly Temple;
Lenin, embalmed, resting nearly
For a century in his tomb,
Once with Stalin removed later
Outside to the Necropolis
By the Kremlin Wall, greets tourists.

[119] Photo taken on April 20, 2014, in Moscow, Russia.

붉은 광장

카잔의 함락
하늘로 치솟는 불꽃으로 축하하며
성 바실리 대성당
성전 의미하며 반갑게 서있네

방부 처리된 레닌
거의 한 세기 그 무덤에 잠들어
관광객들을 맞이하네
한때 함께 했던 스탈린
나중 크렘린 궁전 담장 옆
공동묘지로 옮겨진 채

PETERHOF PALACE[120]

A white screen of the Grand Cascade
With shining figures silhouettes,
The palace descrying the Gulf.

Samson rips the lion's jaws hard,
As triumphant over Sweden
At the pond of the Sea Channel,
Screaming water in agony.

---

[120] Photo taken on May 1, 2014, in Peterhof, Saint Petersburg, Russia.

페테르고프 궁전

번쩍이는 사람들로 된
그랜드 폭포의 하얀 스크린
만 바라다보는 궁전
윤곽 보여주네

삼손
스웨덴에게 의기양양하듯
바다통로 연못에서
사자의 입 크게 찢자
고통에 물로 절규하네

SAGRADA FAMILIA[121]

A vision of a bookseller
Building a church by donations
Sufficed Gaudi's intuition
To Sagrada Familia,
In being built for the long years
With the Nativity facade
In liveliness and the Passion
Facade of grave crucifixion.
Righteous conviction outlasts death.

---

[121] Photos on page 274 taken on September 20, 2010, at Sagrada Familia in Barcelona, Spain.

사그라다 파밀리아

기부로 교회 지으려는
한 서적상의 이상
가우디의 직관을 충족시켜
사그라다 파밀리아 되었네

오랜 세월동안
예수 성탄 정면 활기차고
열정 정면 십자가에 못박힌 예수로 엄숙하게
짓고 있네

바른 신념 죽음을 능가하니

Nativity facade of Sagrada Familia in Barcelona

Passion facade of Sagrada Familia in Barcelona

ALHAMBRA[122]

Intricate carvings of the hall
Of the Abencerrajes lead
In the feud of two families
To tragedy or rejoicing,
Mariano Fortuny's painting
Or Cherubini's opera;
A parabolic array of
Water merges in the channel
With a hypnotic reverie
Just in the Generalife.

[122] Photos on page 278 taken on September 26, 2010, in Alhambra, Spain.

알함브라

아벤세라헤스 홀
미묘한 조각
두 가문의 반목으로
비극이나 환희,
마리아나 포트니 그림이나
체루비니 오페라로 안내하네

헤네랄리페에선
물의 포물선 줄지어
수로와 만나네
최면의 몽상으로

Hall of Abencerrajes of Alhambra in Granada

Generalife of Alhambra in Granada

BLUE HALL[123]

Blue Hall of Stockholm City Hall
Has been reddish as its own bricks,
Not blue against the social norm,
Planned to be blue as the ocean
But left unfinished in red bricks
With adorable, cozy warmth,
Fitted for the Nobel banquet
In the coldness of December.

[123] Photo taken on May 10, 2014, in Stockholm, Sweden.

블루 홀

스톡홀름 시청 블루 홀
사회통념처럼 푸르지 않고
자신 벽돌처럼 늘 불그스레해

바다처럼 푸른색 계획했지만
붉은 벽돌로 끝내지 않은 채
사랑스럽고 아늑한 따스함으로
십이월 추위의 누벨 만찬에 꼭 맞게

COMPASSIONATE DECEPTION[124]

Just in front of the Tre Kronor,
A comely lass approached to me,
Asking with a smile on her face
Just to sign for the handicapped.
I nodded and took her paper,
Listed for name, place, signature,
And donation sum in krona.
I just had fifty-euro notes.
She cried out, "I have enough change!"
Receiving one, she gingerly
Started walking away from me.
My bellowing "Change?" halted her.
A few coins and one ten-dollar!
Ah, compassionate deception.

---

[124] Photo taken on May 10, 2014, at the Tre Kronor in Stockholm, Sweden.

연민의 속음

트리 크루룰 바로 앞
아리따운 아가씨 미소지으며
내게 다가와 장애인 위한
서명 부탁했네

끄덕이고 받아 든 서류엔
이름, 주소, 서명 그리고 크로나 기부금
내겐 오십 유로 지폐뿐
그녀 외쳤네
"거스름 돈 충분히 있어요!"
한 장 받자 그녀 조심스레
나에게서 떠나기 시작했네
내 "거스름 돈?" 외침에 멈춰 선 그녀
동전 몇 개와 십 달러 한 장!
아, 연민의 속음이여

LUCERNE[125]

Mount Pilatus, overlooking
Lake Lucerne and River Reuss
With the Kapellbrücke spanned in wood,
Kneads celestial serenity.

The rock cliff in Glacier Garden
Shelters the Lion Monument,
A lion impaled with a lance
Taking his last moment with grace,
Showing the unfadable scene,
Swiss faith and virtue reflected.

---

[125] Photos on page 286 taken on May 23, 2014, in Lucerne, Switzerland.

루체른

루체른 호수, 로이스 강
강에 걸쳐 있는 나무 다리 카펠뷔르케
내려다보는 필라투스 산
절묘한 평온함 빚어내네

빙하정원 바위절벽 자리잡은
사자기념비,
창에 찔린 채 마지막 순간
품위 있게 맞이하는 사자,
스위스 신의와 덕 반영하며
잊을 수 없는 광경 보여주네

Kapellbrücke in Lucerne, Switzerland

Lion Monument in Lucerne, Switzerland

JUNGFRAU[126]

Jungfrau lifts her veil of cirrus
And stands in white to find her mate
To walk with on the Aletsch lawn,
In aid of Mönch and Eiger.
Who will walk down the aisle with her?

126 Photo taken on May 25, 2014, on the way to Mönchsjoch Hut in Switzerland.

융프라우

융프라우
자신의 새털구름 베일 들어올려
하얗게 단장하고
뮌히와 아이거 도움에
알레치 잔디 위 함께 걸을
자신의 짝 찾으려 하네
누가 그 길 그녀와 함께 할까?

BOSPORUS STRAIT[127]

Black Sea and Sea of Marmara
Interfuse in Bosporus Strait,
Dividing Asia and Europe,
With Istanbul separated.

From Menelaus of Sparta,
Helen and Paris fled to Troy
On the Dardanelles Strait between
The Aegean and Marmara;
Homer sang Iliad and more.

[127] Photo taken on August 15, 2013, in Istanbul, Turkey.

보스포루스 해협

흑해와 마르마라해
이스탄불 갈라놓아
아시아와 유럽으로 나누는
보스포루스 해협에 섞이네

스파르타 메넬라오스로부터
헬레네와 파리스,
에게와 마르마라 사이
다르다넬스 해협에 자리잡은
트로이로 달아났지
호머 노래 불렀지, 일리아드 그리고 더 많은

ST. PETER'S BASILICA[128]

Obelisk at Nero's Circus
Witnessed brutal crucifixion
And Peter's upside-down demise
And observes devotees and sightseers
In front of the Basilica,
The resting place of Saint Peter,
Built on the catacombs, transformed
From Nero's Circus in ruins.

---

[128] Photo taken on October 2, 2009, at St. Peter's Basilica in Vatican City.

성 베드로 대성당

네로 광장에서
잔혹한 십자가형과
피터의 거꾸로 맞이한 죽음
목도했던 오벨리스크,

성베드로 잠들어 있는
폐허 된 네로 광장 변해 된
지하묘지 위에 세워진
대성당 앞에서
독실한 신자와 관광객 지켜보네

Message from the Author

I love You! 그림비.

-81. 5주년 결혼이
회상

Dear Readers,
May your mind and soul be free.
Brighten the universe
With your love and smiles.

CPSIA information can be obtained
at www.ICGtesting.com
Printed in the USA
BVHW020527231118
533726BV00018B/917/P